STEPHEN SANTIAGO REYNOLDS

FROM A BUSH WING

Notes of an Alaska Wildlife Trooper

Editor: Judy Raymond Reynolds
Cover photo by Jeff Babcock

Copyright ©2012 by Stephen Santiago Reynolds

ISBN-10: 1475283296
ISBN-13: 9781475283297

All rights reserved. No part of this publication may be reproduced in any form or by any means without the written permission of the author/publisher.

Portions of chapters 1, 3, 8, 10, 12, 16, 23, and 24 appeared in similar form in Beyond the Killing Tree, A Journey of Discovery, Epicenter Press, 1995 (all rights are now owned by the author). Portions of chapters 7 and 9 appeared in the International Game Warden magazine. Shortened portions of other chapters have appeared in bi-monthly columns published in the Siskiyou Daily News of northern California.

In memory of my cousin,

Lt. Kenneth Dean Smith

B-24 Liberator Pilot with the 371st Bomber Squadron, U.S. Army Air Forces, shot down by Japanese Zekes in the Southwest Pacific, July 5, 1944. Missing in action.

You and your brothers were my heroes, Dean.

And for my children:

Stephen, Coleman, Charles, Cynthia, Karen and Susan

ACKNOWLEDGMENTS

There are some folks I want to thank: One of them is my friend **Don Peek** who suggested several years ago I write a book about flying the Alaska Bush.

My wife, **Judy Reynolds,** has always been the first reader of my writing, and for this book she was instrumental in getting me to return to it after I put it on the back burner for several years, helping to edit it in a professional way and taking a loving interest in general. It doesn't get any better than that.

Ann Chandonette, a talented writer and editor, who unselfishly gave time to my manuscript in its earlier stages, believed in the work, and pushed for publication. Thanks, Ann, wherever you are.

Some other writer friends, brilliant in their own genre, have offered and tendered their support: **Pamela Wallace, Nick Jans,** and **Jean Aspen**.

I also wish to thank Captain **Jeff Babcock**, AST (Ret.), dba Alaska Creative Photography, who has given permission to use his photograph taken on Colony Glacier.

Finally, thanks to those pilots I have known over the years who in some way shaped my destiny or caused me to develop the correct mental attitude—although I didn't always exhibit that attitude. They would not be willing to accept that they were better at starting or finishing the flight than anyone else (but they were—for the most part, and in the long run):

Herbert Ingram, Dick Brown, Fred Fox, Jack Allen, Phil Conner, Bill Griffin, Bob Curtis, Stan Frost, Joe Brantley, Ron Samsal, Ray Tremblay, and Howard Bowman.

CONTENTS

PREFACE 1

PART ONE: BEGINNINGS 5
1. Alone In the Cockpit, Thumb on the Chart 7
2. First Impressions 15
3. A Taste of the North Country 21

PART TWO: THE ARCTIC 27
4. With Harry on the Koyukuk 29
5. Hallucinations 37
6. Building Flight Time. 43
7. The Polar Bear Hunts 49
8. Escape from the Chandalar 53
9. Takahula Ice 59
10. The Wolfers 63
11. Lake of Grace 69

PART THREE: THE RIVER COUNTRY 73
12. Among the River People 75
13. The Bethel Experience 83
14. Pilot's Code of the North 91
15. Giving up the Search 95
16. The Hunters 99
17. Wheels on Water 105
18. Little Joe's Worst Day 109
19. Unscheduled Pit Stop 117

PART FOUR: THE ALASKA PENINSULA 121
20. Wind, Rain, and Darkness 123
21. Yantarni Canyon Rescue 129
22. A Sandy River Mother's Day 135
23. Bad Bob and His Flying Machines 139
24. The Sting 145
25. Wilderness Stakeouts 153

PART FIVE: ENDINGS 159
26. The Broken Dragonfly 161
27. Flying Bricks and Boiled Shirts 167
28. Family Outing 173
29. Attitudes 179

EPILOGUE. 185

PREFACE

Herein are accounts of some Alaskan bush pilots at our worst and best, and true happenings as I experienced them myself or saw them vividly through the eyes of others. A thread runs through this book that has more to do with safety, judgment, and making decisions, rather than simply flying.

Whether tragic, humorous, or surrounding the simple beauty of flight, there is something that jumps out in many of these chapters—how *not* to fly or abuse the privilege of flying. If you are a pilot, you might see some familiar forms—or, better yet, you might think you are looking into a mirror. And if you learn how to improve your own safety record from one or more of these events, then this effort will have been worthwhile...for you, for your friends and families, and for me.

— Stephen Santiago Reynolds
Loon Lake
Talkeetna, Alaska

"Escape may be checked by water and land,
but the air and the sky are free...."

— Dædalus to Icarus

PART ONE: BEGINNINGS

"...It is not the visions but the activity which makes you happy, and the joy and glory of the flyer is in the flight itself."
— Isak Dinesen

CHAPTER ONE

Alone in the Cockpit, Thumb on the Chart

I hear a Piper Super Cub. You do not mistake those sounds that have been a part of you for so long.

From where I live in Alaska, I have agreed to fly an airplane up from Odessa, Texas for a friend who has bought it sight-unseen. Here just outside Odessa it is ten-thirty, and I've been waiting for the fog to lift all morning. A cowboy is flying the little Piper PA-18 Super Cub in from out on a farm or ranch somewhere. I'm wanting to get going. All morning it's been just me and a used airplane dealer—I'll call him Smilin' Jack—in the cramped office of the hangar; stale odor of cigarettes, pot of shallowing coffee made yesterday, thick, like scalded ink, stenching the air. Jack is short and fat and grins too much, and there are ketchup stains on his white shirt. I wander around outside looking at the weeds for something to do, and to escape Jack's incessant jabbering about deals he's made in Mexico and other places, tales causing me to want to check this airplane over even closer than I had originally planned. It is quiet out in the humid weeds. I peer into the fog and think, *With good luck I'll soon be comfortably situated in the cockpit of the small plane, heading north, and in a few days I'll be a billion miles north of this place.* There's a homesick feeling you get when you are stuck in a place and long to be somewhere else.

I hear a Piper Super Cub in the distance (you do not mistake those sounds that have been a part of you for so long). The fog is burning off and the chattery little plane drops in on the sod strip and lands. The cowboy climbs out and I take him aside and say, "Look, you and I are brothers in a way—we both love to fly; tell me what you don't like about this airplane." He says it's a dream—a perfect little puddle jumper. Well, I check it over carefully anyway, of course, for rips and dings and dents and leaks.

I find only one thing wrong with this airplane—well, two things: It has no radio, thus no way to communicate with control towers and flight service stations along the way for weather and conditions, and it has no navigational aids. Texas to Alaska by the seat of your pants.

I get out my World Aeronautical Chart and draw a line straight through to Lethbridge, Alberta. This gives me a general directional line to wander back and forth on through mountain passes and via small towns where I will refuel. Then I take out my sectional charts and draw specific direct routes from place to place. I recheck it all—it will be a bit different without a radio, electric compass, and homing devices. This will be thumb-on-the-chart all the way; matching the terrain with the paper, taking note of railroads and highways, small towns and rivers, and odd features; and using the telephone when I fuel to file flight plans and check on the weather ahead. It isn't exactly a daring venture, like Lindbergh crossing the Atlantic solo, but I feel a kinship with him and the barnstormers of old. Peaceful flight, low altitude, close to things discernible; wave at the farmer in the field, read the name of the small towns on their water towers, land on the back roads for a break, sleep under the wings.

Into the skies of the West Texas plains—*El Llano Estecado*—the day turns to blue and white. Bright. I dogleg up through New Mexico, familiar terrain to the sand in my veins. I was raised here and spent over ten years as a game warden in much of the backcountry I am flying over. High desert—the lowest place in New Mexico is 3,600 feet above sea level. I follow the Pecos River, a little mudhole of a creek when compared to rivers almost anywhere else, but it must have been a sight for parched eyes in those old days of wagon tracks and thirsty mules. Up the east bank I fly and drop in on a familiar ranch road south of Fort Sumner to stretch and relieve myself. I remember an old rancher lady to the east of here who said, when I asked if she liked pronghorn antelope steaks, "I'd just as soon eat an old yaller dog." In the late 1800's this was Billy the Kid's haunts. He's buried just north of here under a granite tombstone chipped by tourists and surrounded by thorny mesquite brush, white sand, and creosote shrubs.

The old-timers said there were homesteaders on every quarter section of this country back around the beginning of the 1900's. Most of them starved out or left for other dream fields—left dugouts and frame houses behind, worn to the resin from the sun and wind. If these old places had ever been painted, you couldn't tell it; the sand scoured the boards clean and left them as gray as the mice. You would be up on the caprock wandering the back roads and here would be a large house sitting out in the middle of a fallow field, wild grass and weeds growing right up to the walls, the paths to the outbuildings reclaimed by sacaton and blue grama. You could step into the breezy rooms of rat feces and shards of scattered glass and wonder about the voices of children. It would strike you that way: families raised here in the midst of Sunday chicken dinners and quilted bedsteads and pictures on the walls. You would have questions in your mind and sense a loneliness about it, yet never gather that you were imposing, for some reason; though you might feel followed as you walked back out to the road.

In the air, north into the Sangre De Cristo foothills of the Rocky Mountains. To the west, Santa Fe; I learned to fly there. It was there I felt the fear.

Flight:
We transcend to that unknown;
a dimension unexplainable by
language, written or spoken;
suspended,
beyond the beyond.

I remember: I am alone in the practice area, three thousand feet above the ground, flying a Cessna 150. I pull the power back while raising the nose, trying to maintain altitude. Higher with the nose. The airplane does not like it—it shudders as the stall-warning buzzer screams louder and louder. The controls feel mushy in my left hand, no response; the nose begins to dip, to break into a stall. I catch it by lowering the nose to gain speed, shoving in power, scooping new life out of the dying wind beneath my wings. Recovery. Practicing stalls—learning to recover, over and over. Try a few power-on stalls: raise the nose, apply power, raise it further, full power, standing on the tail, hanging by the propeller, shudder, shudder, shudder, BREAK to the right! Drop the nose, catch it. Okay, do it again.

As a student pilot, there's something I am not liking about all this. In fact, why am I paying good money for airplane rental to tease a mortal fear? It's a fear that has just developed. I am afraid of the airplane now. If a student pilot doesn't overcome this stage in his training, he may never get back behind the controls. I decide it is a waste, all of it. I fly back to the airport, land, taxi, park, tie it down, and call my instructor, Dick Brown, who is also one of my fellow officers and only one of two pilots with the New Mexico Game and Fish Department. "Dick, I don't think I want to continue with this."

"Why?"

We meet for coffee.

"All of a sudden I just got scared up there, Dick. It's the stalls. I think, what if I don't recover? You know...what if I get into a spin and can't recover?"

Dick does not talk about it. He says, "C'mon." We go out to the airport, get the rental plane, and fly out to the practice area. I've never been in a spin. The FAA does not require spin instruction. Too bad, they should. Dick takes the controls, climbs into an aggravated stall, and puts it in a spin—like a revolving single-leafed seed, down we go. Two revolutions, smooth recovery.

"Now, you do it."

I am excited, laughing; nervous, like when you were a kid and your dad was running along with you while you were trying to ride a bicycle for the first time...and then you realize you are balanced by yourself.

The little Cessna does not want to spin, it wants to fly; you have to make it spin. Power off; nose up, higher; shuddering stall; controls full back; full left aileron, full right rudder—total cross-control—it breaks over and spins. I am pointed toward the revolving earth. Hold it in full cross-control to keep it in the spin; once around, twice around; neutralize the controls (relax), neutralize the rudder pedals; add power; recover. The plane flies. Like a paper airplane, wants you to turn loose of it, let it catch itself.

Climb back up, do it again, lined out far above a highway for reference. This time do one-and-a-half spins, end up going the other direction—precision. Go back up, do it again, this time two-and-a-half revolutions. Precision. Back up; three full spins. We are having fun above the high Santa Fe desert, Dick and I. My fear of the unknown is gone. I now know the sensation of, the configuration of, the ultimate result of the stall/spin. I am balanced by myself and riding the bicycle down the street without fear of falling.

Flying is a blood thing. You learn to fly, and somewhere you overcome the initial fear; then it's a have-to thing. Not a lot else matters. It becomes a pastime, a hobby, possibly the love of your life. If you're not flying, you're down at the airport jawing with the pilots or hangar-flying, and looking at airplanes, caressing the lines and outlines, and whiffing av-gas. If you're not flying, you're there on the ramp alone, like an old tar without a ship looking out to sea.

༄

Into Colorado and back on track. I overnight where I can, where darkness overtakes me, where planning dictates. We Alaska pilots do not think of the "Lower 48" states as a place to get into trouble, just a place on the charts full of roads and railroads, somewhere to push on through to reach real flying country up in the wilds of Canada and Alaska. But on the second day—an afternoon of transition from mid-Wyoming to mid-Montana—I do something that makes me feel dumb, and after several years of flying by that time, I know the consequences of being dumb.

The weather in Lewistown, Montana looks to be good, broken clouds and a few rain showers. I will end up there just before dark. But during the three-and-a-half-hour flight the weather changes a bit, and I see that the Big Snowy Mountains clumped up ahead are blue-black with rain. With it getting late, I can be stupid and push through on course anyway, or I can circumvent the mountains by following the roads and railroads for better reference, most likely placing me into Lewistown after dark, and low on fuel. Not smart either. In flying, it is usually a combination of things that gets you into trouble. In this case, darkness, fuel, and a few other miscalculations.

I intersect the abandoned railroad bed near Ryegate (there's a small landing strip there, which I ignore) and turn west up the Musselshell River to Harlowton where the low, ragged clouds and rain drive me down to a few hundred feet above the ground at the edge of town, almost too low to tell which street turns into the highway going north. But I find it and head in that direction through Judith Gap. I am experimenting right now, wondering if I can see better through the rain and darkness with my prescription sun glasses or without glasses at all; my clear glasses are back out of reach behind the rear seat in the baggage compartment. I need the light on in the cockpit to follow the chart, but I need it off to clearly follow the wet pavement, shiny with a few auto headlights. If things get really bad, I guess I could land on the pavement. At least that would be better than the escarpment of a dark mountainside, provided there are no power lines or eighteen-wheelers in the way.

Flying through the Gap country with white knuckles, I think: *Someday I'll come back and fly this route in the daylight, and it will scare me even worse—will scare me to see with clear glasses what I flew by, around, over, and through while in the black night rain with my shades on.*

I turn east at a road intersection west of Lewistown. An airport light will be there somewhere soon, soon, soon…it has to be. Yes! The relief is at least as profound as Lindbergh's seeing the lights of Paris, France in 1927. Fear knows no boundaries; it flows equally into the pulses of heroes or blind game wardens. I splash through the black puddles of a rain-soaked runway and taxi to a tie-down space. I shut down the engine and listen to the rain drumming on the wings. Maybe this is how white water rafters feel after they reach the restful pools beyond the wild rapids. I think about the dangers of flying. Someone called it "hours and hours of boredom, with a few moments of sheer terror." That someone had been there. That night—later that night in the old hotel there in Lewistown—it feels good to be safe in the feathers, out of the clouds.

From Montana and on into Canada I bypass the big airports: Great Falls, Lethbridge, Calgary, Edmonton. I land at the uncontrolled ones, where I don't need a radio: Cutbank, Red Deer, Whitecourt. Now into the wilderness of western Alberta—this is more like it! I follow the winding rivers, outlines of distant peaks and ridges, shapes of lakes below. New experiences for the little red Cub, but she's grinding along, doing the best she can with no electronics and with a magnetic compass that reads thirty degrees off-course on good days. We follow the flight routes, imaginary paths, thumb on the chart, and leave the winding, dusty, doglegging Alcan Highway to the truckers and tourists.

My move to Alaska several years before had been made by driving that highway. It took over a week just to navigate the 1,100 miles of dirt road through here. Wife, four kids, two cats, rocking chair, saddle, Ford sedan with U-Haul trailer. I think that drive up the Alcan was not so unlike my great-grandparents in their 1885 trek from West Virginia to Oklahoma: big mule team-powered prairie schooner built by creative hands—he was a wheelwright—white oak timber slung underneath for wheel repairs; ten kids aboard. Stop at a creek once a week if you can find one, break out the tubs, scrub clothes and take baths. West, west, into Texas, then north across the Red River; break sod on the wind-exhausted plains; build a house, a home, a life. Those children grew up and left, drifted away, like awns of wild grass carried on a fall wind—all of them—my father's father's generation (the kids in the wagon). I reflect that I didn't know where that forgotten place was until my retirement years. We found it buried under fence rows and the reclaiming prairie grass in south-central Oklahoma. There were families still there from those days.

Of four days in the cockpit, these two days are the longest. Twelve hours on the tachometer for each; that's a long time piloting by dead reckoning. Good weather, broad sky, big country, as I fly north, north, west, west (Anchorage is as far west as Honolulu) over the boreal forests and deep rivers draining north into the Mackenzie and the Yukon. Four thousand miles beyond the weeds of the little airstrip outside Odessa, Texas.

The little red Piper Cub floats above the endless forests as if suspended on a stationary string. Time is space, it does not move; there is no past, no future, only here and now.

CHAPTER TWO

First Impressions

The flight was just a turn around the pattern, and it couldn't have been more than ten minutes or so; it's funny how a few minutes can last a lifetime.

Summer night flights in Alaska can be some of the smoothest when the air is cool and stable. In the Interior it may be almost dark at two in the morning, but you can still see light along the horizon. It is then the night sky is resting, it seems, calling a time-out, and you hang in the air as though stationary at the end of a quiet pendulum.

Emerson said, "In every landscape the point of astonishment is the meeting of the sky and the earth...." It's true, even the late night landscape has its point of astonishment. There are no bumps then in that placid sky. But if you want a bump, you can create one by turning to the left or right through the compass, cutting your own wake burble. It gives you a bit of a *whooomp* like when you strike an easy wave in a boat on a quiet, untroubled lake.

It's these unobtrusive flights at night that give you a tranquil feeling like rain on the roof, or the sense experienced when you stop in the woods to listen during a heavy snowfall, and all you hear is the tapping of the snowflakes on your collar, and it seems that everything else on earth has paused and is listening too. I think in the snowfall there is a true peace shared by all things experiencing the moment: the trees, the birds, the land...even the air itself. There is something akin to it in night flight. You may not think so with the sound of the engine, but the engine is a part of it. In fact, the airplane is a part of it, as though it were alive, and you are close to it then: the airplane, the sky, and the mountains. The constancy of the engine throb and the soft glow of the instrument lights help to create a euphoria of sorts. And you feel finally that there may be a truth to it—that the airplane is alive and sharing your thoughts.

※

I wanted to fly as far back as 1942 when I was five years old—wanted to sail off the garage roof with a handkerchief for a parachute, just to experience the sensation I knew must be there for the trying. My cousin, Dick Robertson, a much older experimentalist at the age of seven, improved upon the foolish handkerchief idea, following it through and using a quarter of an old bed sheet, vaulting off the garage in splendor to the cheers of the neighborhood kids, only to drop like a sack of potatoes to the hard ground. I see him in my mind's eye, folded up on the ground in a sitting position, the useless sheet draped around him, crying in his angry, silent manner as though it had been a great defeat. In his mind it was, I think now. He was determined to overcome the failure.

I remembered Dick being seriously hurt, and it's a wonder he hadn't been, but later family talk about the episode makes no mention of it, only what a silly thing it was. For me it seems there was an agony there though, even more pronounced than the physical pain. Nor, I'm certain, does Dick regard it now as entirely foolish—it was something else.

Dick and I, we had this thing about floating in or flying through the air, and it didn't ever seem foolish to us, especially with all the excitement of the war. Our older cousin, Dean, was a bomber pilot somewhere in the Southwest Pacific, and we couldn't wait to hear the stories he would tell on his return. But he didn't return. And even though Dean's mother always had hope and went to the post office for many years after looking for a letter from him, the rest of the family finally accepted that he was gone. None of us knew what happened to him until sixty years later when the Internet made it possible for me to learn what had taken place. I was able to locate and talk to an old pilot in his squadron who had watched Dean's B-24 go down south of Yap Island, Japanese Zeke fighters strafing the burning bomber all the way to the choppy sea. Five of the eleven men on board were seen to bail out, but the life rafts dropped to them were not found by searchers the next day.

First Impressions

~

Uncle Herbert gave my older sister Ann and me our first ride in an airplane. The small airport lay on the west mesa, the other side of the Rio Grande River from Albuquerque. My sister told me not to look down, "Because it will make you sick," she said, but I looked anyway. The flight was just a turn around the pattern, and it couldn't have been more than ten minutes or so; it's funny how a few minutes can last a lifetime. I remember looking down at the ant hills. You could see them from high up, large round circles like craters on the moon. Out on that flat New Mexico desert of burnt sand and blue sage, with sparse clumps of what we call buffalo grass, the harvester ant hills all had circles around them—areas sometimes ten feet across totally devoid of grass, weeds, or any other sign of growth. Sacrifice zones, in a way, like where cattle gather around a watering hole or salt lick and eat the grass down to nothing. Anyway, it was those circles on the moon, the ant hills, that got my attention; and they're all I remember about the flight except the little silver low-wing Ercoupe we flew in. Every plane I saw after that I compared to Uncle Herbert's 1940 Ercoupe.

That was in 1944 when I was about seven years old. The little Ercoupe wasn't exactly a P-40 Warhawk, or a Navy Corsair, or a P-38 Lightning, but it was all silvery metal just like a lot of those fighter planes were, and it seemed big to me. I hadn't been up close to any of the fighter planes, only seen them high over town lacing the sky, circling and practicing dog-fighting maneuvers. The Ercoupe seemed equally fast and sleek, and as far as my friends were concerned, I'd probably been in something like the Warhawk or the British Spitfire maybe, the way I described the ride to them. None of them had ever been in an airplane. Much later I saw an Ercoupe once again, and couldn't believe it at first—didn't want to—it looked like something out of a box of Cracker Jacks compared to the large fighters.

After the war, I used to sneak into the fenced areas at Kirtland Air Base, east of town. There was a boneyard out there—a graveyard they called it—for moth-balled World War II airplanes, all the old fighters and bombers that came back from the war, miles of them lined up, row after row, in the hot desert sun and tumbleweeds.

On our bikes my friends and I would ride out to the desert east of the base, slip through a hole in the fence and explore. We would sit in the turrets playing gunner, blasting those sneering devils diving at us in Japanese Zeroes or German ME 109s, re-living the dramatic movie renditions, fresh in our minds, of the Pacific or European battles—the ones with John Wayne, Errol Flynn, or Ronald Reagan; only there was no smell of popcorn here, no cool, dark, deep-piled movie theater with ushers using discreet flashlights. This, by God, was the real thing, out here in the hot sun of the blue Pacific, or above the clouds over the coast of France, fighting the enemy, burning off the aggression.

In the pilot's seat of the old Boeing Flying Fortresses and Consolidated Liberators, I would drive the controls for miles, shouting orders to my friends who were busy shouting their own orders somewhere in the belly or back in the tail-gunner's turret. There was the smell of grease in the hot compartments and claustrophobic gunner bubbles, and everything was metal, not shiny, but drab with a universal olive yellow paint. The only shiny things were the dog tags the men had left behind. There were names you never heard of, and we would try to find the oddest ones and save those, or shout at someone, "Hey, over here! Listen to this one!" And it was noisy in those old bombers as we tore our way through them from one end to the other, re-fighting the war of our heroes.

Sometimes I went out there alone, but then it was different. Because it was quieter, I could sit in the pilots' seats, maneuver the controls, and imagine the sense of flight that I saw in the movies or newsreels—rumbling engines droning across the high Pacific or the Atlantic or the English Channel—and convince myself I was a war hero like my cousins Dean, or Malcolm, or Fred, three brothers larger than life in my memory, who either left their dog tags in their old tank destroyers or bombers at the end of the war...or kept them around the neck forever, like Dean, in his B-24 at the bottom of the Pacific.

As for my cousin Dick (the young parachutist with the bed sheet), he went on to MIT. Then, since he couldn't find the sort of excitement he craved there, he quit and joined the army and eventually became a sergeant wearing the green beret of the Special Forces, and later a master sergeant with the 82nd Airborne—no doubt a master too at jumping out of airplanes with real parachutes and serious thoughts in mind. He wrote me about his first jump from a C-130 Hercules over Japan: "Launching into the 130 knot slipstream, I hold my breath the whole three minutes and twelve hundred feet to the ground and land softly, feet, side, shoulder, in a Japanese farmer's pea patch. I roll over and see the beautiful blue blossoms and my Irish classmate who has landed nearby figures we have died and this is our funeral."

※

For me, there wouldn't be any jumping out of airplanes; I wanted to fly them.

CHAPTER THREE

A Taste of the North Country

Maybe we return to the old fears of our childhood as we age, when we are safe once again from the dangers, or are simply thankful to have made it this far and wonder how we did.

I wouldn't get another airplane ride until the summer of 1957 when I was nineteen and headed for an Alaskan summer job. The U.S. Fish and Wildlife Service was hiring most of its Alaska Territorial stream guards from the states, paying their way up and back from Seattle. For a college student fresh out of the desert, this was a free trip to paradise for the summer. The midnight flight out of Seattle was on a Pacific Northern Airways Super Constellation, a state-of-the-art way to fly in those days—seven hours from Seattle to Anchorage, the four big radial engines trying to lull you to sleep.

There were fourteen of us to be indoctrinated on a single day in Anchorage, trying to absorb all there was to know about the commercial salmon fisheries, the laws we would enforce, first aid, survival techniques, report writing, repairing stoves and lanterns and outboard motors, and operating small skiffs on the ocean waves. It's hard for me to believe now that the Federal Government thought this was adequate training for a bunch of young guys from the lower forty-eight states. There were few, if any, stream guards hired from Alaska.

We flew out of Lake Hood in a twin-engine amphibian Grumman Goose: three stream guards and all our gear, with just enough room for us to lie on top of the tents, outboard motors, groceries and baggage, as we peered down through the windows at the vast coastal wilderness drifting by. No horizons from this angle, only a downward view into tundra, spruce, birch, willows, lakes and bogs. Too much, and too fleeting, to impress the mind with anything more than the newness of a strange country. The inside of the Goose was painted in the olive drab World War II paint of those old boneyard bombers, and the twin Pratt and Whitney Wasp engine, close by outside the porthole I was looking through, throbbed with power along with its twin on the other wing.

The airport at Kenai was then a dirt strip in the tundra. We bounced along in the dust and pulled up to a wooden hangar where we let off one man and his gear. I didn't envy him; we were still in civilization, in my opinion. Then we were off the ground to Port Dick, beyond the boardwalk village of Seldovia, where the brown sea of Cook Inlet began to broaden green and clean itself of silt. There we off-loaded the next stream guard. He was luckier. I detected my first aroma of wilderness there. It poured through the open hatch of the bobbing Grumman—a scent of spruce, alder and kelp.

It was late afternoon by the time we touched down in salt spray far up the East Arm of Nuka Bay, beyond the Pye Islands, a fjord along the outer rim of sea coast still attached to the Kenai Peninsula thumb. The pilot, a young, fussy transplanted Canadian, lowered the Grumman's gear legs, dodging real and imagined black rocks off the beach with the use of the big tail rudder. With the skillful hand/eye coordination of an artist, he alternated power between the two radial engines as he lowered the gear and drove the old seaplane up onto the sandy shore near the mouth of Delight Creek, my assigned post. There were no special last minute instructions for me after we off-loaded my equipment; the pilot's job was simply to get me here. Although he worked for the U.S. Fish and Wildlife Service, he didn't show much interest beyond "driving the bus." He answered my questions with grunts and shrugs, and likely was in a hurry to get home to Anchorage for supper.

Moments later I stood alone on the windblown beach, a mound of gear stacked behind me, and listened to the drone of the Grumman's engines fading into the distance. There was the strange sensation then of wanting the sound of those engines to return. It was a lonely place at first, but later, in one of my letters home, I would say, "You really don't have to be alone if you imagine that you aren't. The best thing is to not think about it." I would remain there for the summer protecting spawning streams and exploring them to their sources while counting salmon. Little did I know that I would touch that same place again 15 years later. By then I was a wildlife officer and pilot with the State of Alaska stationed in the bush village of McGrath on the Kuskokwim River, but assigned for a week or so assisting with the commercial fishery enforcement in Cook Inlet.

This was after the big earthquake of 1964—the fault line running right through Nuka Bay—and the country had changed geographically since I last saw it, the landmass having dropped between five and seven feet. In addition, the tsunami caused by the quake had roared into the fjords of the Outer District ninety to a hundred feet high. There remained little sign of those lowland features I had spent the summer of 1957 exploring.

But it was still a wilderness, and destined to stay that way with the eventual establishment of the Kenai Fjords National Park. There is no wilder country, even today. In 1957 I didn't doubt my abilities in such a place; maybe I should have, but sometimes youthful confidence carries you through. Now that I've lived and survived in some of the wildest places of Alaska, from the Arctic to the panhandle, I shudder a little at what I didn't know in those early days about survival and precautions against an untimely death. I sometimes have bad dreams now about slick ice and conked-out boat motors, deep water, and errant bears. I didn't have the wisdom to know what to be frightened of then. Maybe we return to the old fears of our childhood as we age, when we are safe once again from the dangers, or are simply thankful to have made it this far and wonder how we did.

༄

After returning from the Alaska adventure in 1957, I spent a couple of years in college, and then ten years as a game warden with the New Mexico Game and Fish Department. Nine years of it were full of adventure, but the last year resembled a zoo when I found myself caged in the head office in Santa Fe. There was a title with the job, but the freedom was gone—turned loose in the hills for nine years, then chained behind a desk. Sack lunch, white shirt and tie. I was thirty-one years old, destined to the four walls of an office for twenty more years until retirement. It was like having to eat sauerkraut and okra every day.

They were recruiting game wardens in Alaska, preferably with law enforcement and wildlife experience. I had run out of back roads and trails in New Mexico. It would be unlikely I would ever run out of them in Alaska, and I didn't ever want to end up in an office again. I had just learned to fly, and I wanted some freedom. I still had memories and dreams of those floatplanes at the U. S. Fish and Wildlife hangar at Lake Hood—most of those same airplanes now belonging to the state. I made application and was later interviewed by phone.

⁂

My first permanent assignment with the Alaska Fish and Game Department is to the village of Anderson, on the road system just north of McKinley Park. It is before the highway has been punched through from Anchorage to Fairbanks, so the road leads to nowhere for now. We buy a small house and get settled in. It's a good place for the kids: The woods and creeks run in all directions from the edge of town. For me, however, it's frustrating at first. There is only one road, running north and south—a big district full of flying hunters and flying hunting guides, and no way to get to them, except by horseback, in some cases. I can catch the train up the Nenana River to Cantwell, borrow a Department of Highways pickup, and patrol what dirt roads there are—out the Paxson Highway or back into the reaches of McKinley Park. The U. S. Park Service has given me keys to their ranger cabins. But my movement is confined without an airplane.

It's the days in Alaska just before the oil money is in the coffers, and we game wardens don't have a lot of equipment. What we have is good, but we don't have much, and must share it around with other districts. Not having an airplane the majority of the time in this district, I need to figure out other ways to cover the country.

I locate some horses to rent from a rancher near Healy. This horseback patrol with pack animals is something I know how to do from my years with the New Mexico Game and Fish Department. In early August I load up two of them, throw my saddle on the other one and set out to spend ten days patrolling the Dall sheep hunting season in the Wood River country east of Mt. McKinley National Park. A significant part of my patrol in New Mexico had been horseback, so I feel at home in the saddle once again.

Aside from some aggressive grizzly bears encountered, I figure the sheep patrol is a success. Every hunter contacted by foot or horseback out there in the woods is worth a hundred checked in the camps along the road system, but I long to be saddled with an airplane. In a Super Cub I can land on these gravel bars and check out more hunter and guide camps in a couple of hours than in a couple of days on the hoof. There's a lot of country to cover.

⁓

In this first Alaska district of mine, I don't have a river boat either, and there are many miles of navigable rivers that have never seen a game warden closer than 2,000 feet above the treetops. The local Episcopal priest, Father John Phillips, is a friend. He lives in the Tanana River village of Nenana, the major jumping-off port for Interior Alaska villages along the Tanana and Yukon rivers. Alaska's only inland railroad crosses the river at Nenana, where the old sternwheelers once based, replaced now by the diesel-powered tugs.

If you live in Nenana and you want to earn some money, you probably work for the Yutana Barge Line or the Alaska Railroad. You probably aspire, if you are a kid, to being a barge line riverboat captain or an engineer on the train or even a bush pilot. You don't think about having a car—at least not back before there are any roads to amount to anything. You think about having a riverboat of your own. It will be maybe twenty-four feet long, narrow, of sturdy timbered plywood and two-by-fours, with a lift for raising the motor while you skim over shallow river bars. You will build the boat yourself, under the tutelage of an old-timer, and the materials and motor you will purchase with firefighting money. In Nenana the flat-bottomed riverboats line the silt bank like rafts of basking alligators along a Louisiana bayou.

Father John owns one of these boats, and we strike a deal. It is a good deal for John and for us: He will loan me his boat and motor two or three days at a time; we will give him a barrel of gas in trade. It gets me out onto the river. What I learn on the river, reading the water, will be of value when I start flying airplanes with floats on my own. Winding, swirling, drift-infested, muddy river; bobbing widow-makers just beneath the surface, anchored trees ready to spear an unsuspecting hull. Watch for the big boils; they're okay, that's where the water's deepest. Read where the big water-volume is likely to flow, cutbank to cutbank. Cutbanks: where spruce tree sweepers lie horizontal, slapping the current.

If you smell bad, get out on the river and blow away the stink, they say. Well, I'm not so sure, but you can blow away the mosquitoes. However, the biting little devils will get you sooner or later; you have to come to shore sometime. I always dope up before pulling into the bank. You only jump ashore and try to tie up a boat or floatplane once without doping up first, to know what it means.

I learn the river. There's a Fish and Game cabin in the Minto Lakes area, not far down the Tolovana River from the village of New Minto. Sometimes I retreat to there from off the muddy Tanana at the end of a day, doing a little pike fishing on the way. Good, white, flaky meat, but watch for the Y-bones. These northern pike throughout lakes of the Minto Flats grow to three and four feet. I don't catch any like that, but it charges the blood just knowing they are there.

Fall time on the Minto Flats. Birch-blazed forest of saffron and burnt sienna. Duck hunters from Fairbanks descend by the floatplane load, pick up their cached riverboats and charge around the bends, hell-bent, blasting through fleeing waterfowl, shotguns blazing. Game warden sitting there with ticket book. Surprise! Take your ticket like a man; thank ol' Father John, amen.

On the Tanana there are treed islands and channels you never see, unless you search them out, but a channel might be narrow and end at a sweeper or shallow bar, so you stick with the best guesses: stay with the deep water, hold with the boils and the cutbanks.

You think there may be great, grassy meadows up beyond the riverbanks, places of sweet cleanness, but there aren't. The ground there is silt, gristed grains of a once river among the ferns and willow and white spruce. Sand, you might call it, but it's finer than that; and there's a humidity in there that fastens itself to you; and the bugs are bad—mosquitos, black gnats and whitesocks that whine and bite—and salt sweat stings the eyes. It is a place to escape from, a strangulation, like the dusty, salt-cedar thicket of a desert. You want to burst out of there, back to the open, blowing coolness of the river.

Up above Tolchakat Slough a river tug is coming down, and from the surface you can see that it lays low upon the river, shoving a bulge of smooth water ahead of the barge. In your skiff you turn to catch the wave, trailing like a whale's wake, bleeding away in wide traces toward a caving shore.

PART TWO:
THE ARCTIC

"Remember that below the sea of clouds lies eternity."
— Antoine de Saint Exupery

CHAPTER FOUR

With Harry on the Koyukuk

Airplanes live. When they are first put together and the spark of energy is added, they are brought to life. And ever after, though they may be shut down and covered with snow on a frozen morning, that energy and life lingers, and you know it....

Two of us are staying at the Bettles Lodge, a large log structure, and the most prominent feature in the Arctic outpost of Bettles Field in the foothills of the wilderness Brooks Range. An old Koyukon Athabascan living down by the river comes to wake us at three in the morning. He says the river has just risen nine feet in the last few hours. This is becoming commonplace—not the river rising nine feet, but people pounding on the door in the middle of the night. It's something I should get used to, Harry says, as long as I'm going to be a wildlife officer in the Alaska Bush. Somebody's always needing something, or maybe they are just drunk, or there's a fight down the road, or a fire maybe. If there's an officer in town, regardless of what he may imagine his own priorities to be, he'll be expected to handle whatever emergency crops up. That's the rule for a state officer in rural Alaska; there is no one else to pass it off to.

But the old man isn't drunk, nor does he wake us just to report the water level—it's our floatplane docked along the river bank. The state Cessna 180 is about to be carried away by the high waters and drifting spruce trees and birch logs.

Bettles Field and the small village of Evansville are two miles upstream from the old original Bettles, an abandoned mining-supply village across the Koyukuk River. From here at Bettles Field, I'm assigned to patrol the opening of the Dall sheep and grizzly bear seasons in the Arctic Brooks Range. It's a wet fall, my first in Alaska after leaving New Mexico to work for the Fish and Game Department. I don't know if the wet weather is commonplace or what. The rivers along the south slope of the Brooks have been running high and muddy since before the first of August when we got here. But, for the last three days it has been raining harder in the headwaters of the Koyukuk's north and middle forks, and the heavy rain is washing the slush of an early snowfall down from the high country.

I haven't yet built up the 200 hours flight time in Alaska to be checked out in state aircraft, so one of the biologists in the northern region—let's just call him Harry, out of consideration—has been sent along to fly the airplane assigned to my patrol, a 1964 Cessna 180 on Edo floats.

Harry is not a good pilot, in my estimation, but he's a Department check pilot and a certified instructor—none of which he should ever have been, I think—so he has been preparing me for a float rating while on patrol (God help us all). I had no inkling it would take a concerted effort on my part over the next year or so to unlearn much of what Harry is teaching me in order to pick up my float rating.

Harry is a reasonable facsimile in appearance to Wiley Post, the around-the-world pilot from back in the thirties: a bit squat and roundishly solid, almost nondescript, and a bit rumpled. Mr. Post, however, had one good eye, which is an improvement over Harry. Not only could Harry use some glasses, in my estimation, but he seems stressed just being in the airplane, especially in snotty weather. He breaks out into a sweat then, and has the interesting habit of constantly wiping his hands on his trousers; first one hand, then the other. Whichever hand he is wiping on his trousers, the other is tightly gripping the controls. First one, then the other...one, then the other.

I think, though, if I had to come up with the single most important reason why Harry is unsuccessful as a good pilot, it would be that he seems to harbor no respect for airplanes; they mean nothing to him, just a manner of conveyance. I've rarely seen anyone like that in the flying business. Most of the pilots I know have a reverence for airplanes—admiring them as things of beauty, elegant machines of clean and perfect lines representing a smooth connection to other sights they value: sky and vistas from the sky, serenity of flight, serenity of light, and extended existence into another dimension. When you own an airplane, or fly the same one continually, it becomes a companion. You talk to it. It reassures you back, takes care of you, and forgives you—up to a point.

Airplanes live. When they are first put together and the spark of energy is added, they are brought to life. And ever after, though they may be shut down and covered with snow on a frozen morning, that energy and life lingers, and you know it; and it will be there until the airplane is augured into the ground or parted out in a boneyard, or forgotten for too long and left alone on the tarmac somewhere—like a pet dog you neglected to feed and water, and for whom you forgot to show a little love and respect.

With an airplane and you, there's a connection between the engine and the heart—a tuning together; and after you've been with each other for a while, there's an understanding between the two of you. Experienced pilots know this; just ask them. They'll tell you also that airplanes will not betray any lie you want to tell. You can lie about some incredible feat that you and your flying machine accomplished; do this in the presence of the craft while both you and whomever you are telling the lie to stand admiring it, and the machine will wallow in the glow of admiration right along with you and the listener. However, therein is the difference. You can lie about the airplane, but you cannot be a liar *to* the airplane.

And this is Harry's problem. He isn't honest with the machine he flies; he doesn't show it that respect. It's a lie when he lets the plane think he's tied it down by simply running a line through the tie-down ring and giving the line a single loop over itself and walking away. "There, I tied you down; that's good enough." And it's a lie with all those other things that need attention when you and the airplane are supposed to be loyal to each other—all single loop lies. "There, I pumped a float compartment; the others are probably OK....There, I strained the fuel on this side; I'll do the other side tomorrow....I made a run-up yesterday, no need to do it two days in a row....I checked the oil a couple of days ago; I know about how much oil this thing burns....Oops, I forgot to roll that HF antennae in before we landed; I'll get another one put on when we get back to town."

You can see I've been impressed with Harry. His attitude and sloppiness give me scant confidence in his instruction on float flying. On the other hand, he doesn't have to be letting me fly. In fact, if you are a pilot, it's not much fun to turn the airplane over to someone else and watch them fly askew to the way you might do it. But it doesn't bother

Harry. And another thing: Because he's not fussy about my handling (or mishandling) of the airplane, I'm comfortable flying it; my landings and takeoffs don't seem any worse than the majority of his. He fights the airplane constantly, trying to bulldoze it up onto the water-planing step, then trying to horse it off the water. It seems to me the thing wants to fly best if you don't try to over-manage it and if it's trimmed correctly to begin with. But, I don't argue with Harry about those things; you don't learn much while arguing, and Harry's the one with the experience here.

I'm in awe of the country, regardless of the constant rain. There are endless miles of wilderness and strings of mountains—the high peaks striking up and out of the boreal forest and tundra hills, steel gray against the greens and the fall shades of scarlet and ochre; the clear lakes and roily rivers, big and small, over every ridge, named and unnamed—country that is absent of human infiltration. The Brooks Range is the last true American wilderness they say, and I agree, even now.

A few weeks prior to leaving New Mexico I had dug up a book by Constance and Harmon Helmricks at the library in Santa Fe. It was about their adventures across the Arctic and in the Brooks Range of the 1940s, and about their homestead cabin on Takahula Lake. This book was somewhat fresh on my mind as Harry and I began my first flights into this vast country. I hadn't mentioned the book to Harry, nor had I remembered the name of the lake in the book, for that matter. And although he was fairly well acquainted with the Brooks Range, Harry was not familiar with a little lake we picked to land on that first day on this assignment. After an hour or so of flying, we noticed the small lake off to west of the Alatna River and landed there—my first landing on still water. There was a small cabin on a knoll at the northeast corner; we taxied over to it and went ashore. It was unlocked, so we went in out of curiosity, as it was an immaculately constructed and well-cared for little cabin and warranted closer inspection. The place looked familiar to me; I couldn't figure it out. Then I saw a note on the table addressed to someone due to be staying there soon, I suppose, as there were boxes of fresh groceries stacked around. The note was signed by "Bud" Helmricks. This was Takahula Lake. Of the hundreds of lakes scattered about the immense Brooks Range, why had we picked this one for a first landing?

Later, Harry and I landed on some lakes on the north slope of the range—bald country on that side; treeless, but livid with the fall colors of dwarf birch, lichens and willow. We've landed on these lakes at will, practicing some landings and takeoffs, checking for hunting and guide camps, of which there are very few, and, oh yes...done a little fishing; just testing the waters for twenty- to thirty-year-old lake trout and seventeen-inch grayling, and seeing after the Arctic char—seeing if they've arrived yet from the salty Beaufort Sea to the north of us.

We fish the mouths and outlets where the grayling, char and lakers seem most prevalent. From there you can look straight up the length of a lake—some of these waters are four and five miles long. I can't help but think, as we stand there swatting mosquitoes and catching fish, how one of these lakes transposed into New Mexico would have three marinas on it and twelve major campgrounds. But no one is there but us, nor do we hear a single airplane in the distance.

୬∽

At Bettles this morning the Koyukuk River has risen nine feet in the last few hours, according to the old man, and our plane is about to be lost. We trot the half-mile or so down to the river, Harry and I, and find that the upriver end of the small dock has broken loose from the bank. The dock, with our plane secured to it, has swung out into the current crossways, the rear line of the dock stretched as tight as a guitar string and ready to snap like a pistol shot at any minute. How the logs, stumps, and full-bodied trees gliding ponderously by have missed colliding with the outstretched dock is a mystery. There are lots of trees adrift, and the dock is situated right in the middle of a bend in the river, the receiving end. Harry shouts over the noise of the rushing water, "We're going to have to move the plane!"

He's right, of course; there's nothing to do but climb in, then try to dodge the floating drift and get off the river. But where to then? We don't talk about it—there isn't time; you can see all there is to know at a glance.

Harry gets in and is ready to start the engine as soon as a clear spot shows in the drift coming down. I stand on the dock ready to release us when he gives the signal. We both watch the river. It is still raining hard, and the sky is ragged with scud and hanging mist and fog. A dark morning, even though here above the Arctic Circle it's normally bright daylight around the clock this time of year.

There's a break in the trashed trees and limbs coming down with the swift current. Harry gives the signal, and I release the loop of line holding us to the dock, giving the plane a shove straight out and climbing on the float as Harry starts the engine, the blast of the prop making it difficult to hold the door open far enough to squeeze my way in. But I'm in then, my slicker wet and dripping, as is Harry's, the moisture and humidity fogging up the inside of the windscreen. I stay busy trying to keep the pilot's side wiped off as Harry taxies with a roar from the lee of the dock, out into the main stream of the rolling, gray-brown froth of current. I'm thinking, *This is exciting business, but what am I doing in here with this half-assed pilot?*

But now Harry is all business: no fretting, no time for it; no wiping of the hands on his trousers. Like a surgeon or an artist, his hand/eye coordination is tuned in to what he's doing while he maneuvers his way across the current to the far side of the river. He makes his way downriver to where he figures he's got enough room for takeoff, whips the plane around, and then carefully turning and weaving while peering upriver for the sign of a break in the debris, he waits, like a trout standing against the current.

There's really no choice; the plane has to come off this river. There's no safe mooring place on either bank. If we hit a stump or log, we'll not only lose the plane, but our lives as well. We don't discuss it—it's apparent without discussion what has to be done. I'm along for the ride, other than keeping the screen cleared of fog and watching for logs: those gray ones, almost the color of river water mixed with overcast.

Harry shoves in the throttle. He's carefully run the prop through its cycles, checked the mag drops, maintained carburetor heat—gradually pushing it forward just ahead of the power—and now he goes for it, pulling the water rudders up once he's got enough directional control with the tail rudder and lined in the right direction. Moving fast across the water and up on the step, he skillfully maneuvers around an errant tree swept into our path as the plane begins to lighten its load on the water. He cocks in the left aileron while maintaining a straight path with the rudder pedals, raises the right float off the water and then the other, and we're in the air. He maintains full power as he banks around the bend in the river—the high spruce trees bordering us on either side—bleeds the flaps off, and only then, once he has his speed up and total control of where he's headed, does he come back on the power, then the prop, and the high whine of the engine settles to the hundred-mile-an-hour hum of a shallow climb out over the trees—the rain heavy on the windscreen. We dodge a low layer of gray clouds in front of us along the hills and head for a lake a few miles to the south of the village to wait out the weather and the river. We're safe now—we and the airplane.

I'm thinking maybe Harry likes this plane after all, to risk everything in the wee hours of a dark morning to save it. I look over and see him wipe his hand on his trouser leg.

CHAPTER FIVE

Hallucinations

What was waiting for him under the expanse of dense clouds, he didn't know, but he hoped and prayed that maybe it was the Yukon River or a large lake—some Godsend of water.

The Bettles Lodge was a roadhouse in the true sense of the word. There were still a lot of them around in the late nineteen-sixties and early seventies—a carryover from the old dog-sled trail days in Alaska. For the most part, these places served good, hearty meals and provided clean sleeping accommodations. Almost any village of more than a hundred people had one when I first arrived, and there were some still located in remote places like Bettles and down on the Kuskokwim River at Bethel.

The meals were served only during certain hours, just like at home. If you showed up late, there might be a chance that you could dig up some leftovers in the kitchen, or the cook might even fix you a hamburger or fried ham sandwich. No menus were provided—the meals were full-course—but what you saw was what you got, and usually you were glad of it.

In these roadhouses there was always a large wooden dining table, free of any frills or table cloth, accompanied by long benches where everyone sat for dinner, like at a boarding house, I suppose. Around this table folks usually gathered for coffee and a chance to smoke and jaw late into the night or when the weather was tough. It was here at the Bettles Lodge dining table where an experienced bush pilot named Callahan told a story of survival I would not forget.

Callahan was a pilot for the local air taxi operator. He said at one time they had an old twin-engine "Bamboo Bomber," a nickname for the 1939 Cessna T-50 Bobcat, which had been used early in WWII as a trainer for the Royal Canadian Air Force before being accepted by the U.S. Army Air Force and Navy. It was a low-wing plane built with wooden spars and ribs and covered in fabric, and could be bought for as little as $600 after the war. In the summer Callahan's Bobcat was on floats, and he would ferry supplies from Fairbanks out to Bettles, north of the Arctic Circle, where he operated off the twisted Koyukuk River. The Koyukuk could be tricky for any airplane but especially a low-wing twin, both for docking and maneuvering for takeoffs and landings. The Bobcat was a workhorse, but a handful.

While returning from Fairbanks with a load of supplies on one of these freight flights, and while Callahan was above the overcast somewhere in the vicinity of the Yukon River, he figured, the number one engine sputtered and quit. The load on board was too heavy to allow single-engine flight, to hold any altitude at all, and the old plane began a quick descent down through the heavy clouds. There had been no pilot reports regarding the enroute weather from Fairbanks, and Callahan only knew that the weather was reported good at Bettles where he planned to land. Flying on top of the clouds isn't dangerous with a twin under normal circumstances, but in this case, with the heavy weight, it was no safer than single-engine flight. What was waiting for him under the expanse of dense clouds, he didn't know, but he hoped and prayed that maybe it was the Yukon River or a large lake—some Godsend of water, and not the mountains that frame both sides of the Yukon on that flight path.

Callahan tried to re-start the dead engine at first, while streaming down through the shroud of clouds, but smartly decided he should feather the prop and ready himself for an emergency landing of some sort. When he finally broke out underneath the overcast, he saw he had a couple of thousand feet of altitude left, which he was thankful for. But there wasn't any long, wide Yukon River, or water of any size in sight, though fortunately he had missed the mountains by being a little to the right of on-course, coming down just beyond the broadening expanse of the Yukon River Flats.

Across the boreal forest choked in spruce and birch, there was but a single, tiny lake in sight in his quickly shallowing descent to the ground, and it was surrounded by trees—his Godsend of water. He would have to go for it. There wouldn't be a second chance, so he needed to make the approach just right. His main concentration was to not overshoot the landing and end up flying the twin into the trees at the far end of the lake, yet maintain an approach speed of 90 miles an hour and not stall it before he got there.

That may be why he wound up too low, and why he caught the tops of the tall spruce trees on the approach end of the lake, putting him into the water certainly, and in one piece, both he and the airplane, but unfortunately upside down, after all the white-knuckle floundering was said and done.

He said his first thought was to just get out of the sinking plane. But then after he was out, still coughing up lake water and trying to catch his breath while on top of the bottoms of the aluminum pontoons, and before he began a swim for the shore, he realized he had better see if he could salvage some emergency gear from inside the airplane. It could be a long wait. The plane hadn't sunk any further and seemed to have stabilized, the floats about ten inches or a foot under water.

Callahan went back down and was able to retrieve an old army duck-feathered mummy bag and a steel survival mirror, but his efforts of diving several times down into the submerged plane sapped his strength, and he began to wish he'd just gone for the shore to start with. Now he was stuck out in the middle of the lake sitting in a foot of cold water.

He convinced himself, after a bit, that he could probably make it to shore. So, abandoning the sodden bedroll, which he now realized would weigh him down if he tried to drag it with him, he struck out for shore, but very quickly knew he wouldn't make it.

How far out he got before he knew that, and how he was able to swim back to the floats, or even find them for that matter, I don't know, nor did he say if he knew himself. He only said he made it back, retrieved the bedroll, and that eventually, in a fit of strength, got inside the soggy thing and wept. For those who know, to be damp and cold and alone in the deep woods as dark settles, and without a fire, is painful. To be stranded in water and unable to reach even those damp, cold woods may likely bring about an early bereavement for the self you know you are losing.

Night came and he waited it out, so totally drained that he must have dozed off and on. The next day he thought searchers might find him—*There would be searchers out, wouldn't there?*—but the weather was miserable for flying, with drizzle and fog, and he heard no airplanes. The gray sky and woods were mute. In his hypothermic condition, he began to sleep more often and for what he thought were longer periods of time. He tried to imagine himself warm, that it was only a fallacy that it was cold where he was, and that it was really very comfortable—that the bedroll was full of heat and he was dry. It was on the third day that he began to hallucinate. At first it was comforting, he said, pleasant images and friends he knew circling about and talking to him in muffled voices.

Then the hallucinations got worse, and it was demons and nightmares in broad daylight. At one time, he said, the nightmares let up and he realized there were people on the shore, finally. They were hollering at him, and he knew with relief that he had been found. But he couldn't understand why his mother was there with the rest—what would she be doing up here in Alaska, all the way from the lower forty-eight states? And then they all began to tell him to swim, that he could make it, that it was only a short way, beckoning him to come on, come on, it's okay, we'll help, it's all right, you can do it, we believe in you. He said he was trying to struggle out of the water-logged bedroll, trying so hard to do it as in a dream, and he knew very well and without doubt they would help him and he must give it his all and that he couldn't expect them to do it for him. He had been raised that way, you know, he said, that the Lord helps those who help themselves; and now his friends and mother were on the shore yelling encouragement, and how could he let them down? He had come fully awake, and felt a strength, and decided he wasn't afraid to try it, and when he was about to do it, he saw his father on shore. Callahan knew then something wasn't quite right, he said, because his father had been dead for some time, and his father wasn't saying anything, just standing there, and it was all of a sudden like the old man was the only real one there on the shore, and how could that be?

It gave him pause to reconsider.

The fourth day dawned clear and sunny. He heard a helicopter. Callahan flashed his steel mirror at it, though it was up high. He had heard and seen other aircraft at different times, but was not convinced they were real. He had flashed his mirror at them too, or thought he had, or maybe it was a dream; but this helicopter *was* real. The observer spotted a glint of something from a lake far below as they were passing, so they investigated, but couldn't believe their eyes—a ghost of a man sitting out in the middle of the lake on the sunken bones of an airplane.

The helicopter landed on shore where they broke out a small survival raft and paddled out to Callahan. They carefully lifted him into the raft. He said his joints felt like fragile glass, and where they touched him it seemed like a thousand needles were being pushed into his flesh. They took him to the shore, and he said he knew it had to be real, that the pilot of the helicopter wept when he saw the condition that Callahan was in—starved gaunt, water-logged, shriveled like a white prune, with deep-set black eyes on a body that was skinny to begin with.

He reasoned—he told us, while at the dining table there in the Bettles roadhouse late that night—he reasoned if the pilot had been simply one of his hallucinations, it was certain the pilot would not have wept. "He didn't even know me, so I knew he had to be real."

CHAPTER SIX

Building Flight Time

The other plane had simply slipped off the steep ridge and flown away like an eagle dropping off a spruce snag and catching the wind under his wings.

Oil had been discovered up on the Beaufort Sea coast at Prudhoe Bay in 1968. During the following winter, before a state trooper was permanently assigned to that country, and prior to any sort of security service, we state officers in the northern region would take a turn of two weeks each providing law enforcement in the oil fields. When divided between all the officers with the State Troopers and the Fish and Game, this duty occurred only once for each of us before increased oil production activity and the pipeline construction required a permanent police officer. My stint was in mid-April of 1970, with spring still a month or so off. We were provided lodging at British Petroleum headquarters which was a small camp of about twenty men near Lake Colleen, not far from the Deadhorse Airstrip. Atlantic Richfield also had a small camp closer to the bay, a few miles to the north. The only other major camp was that of Frontier Sand and Gravel who was building the roads and pads for the well-sites scattered about. Other than the drill rigs themselves, there were no major construction projects at that stage in the discovery—a lull before the storm. The camps were quiet and the men well-mannered generally (a troublemaker was simply put aboard an airplane and given a one-way ticket to town). At Deadhorse the Wien Airlines terminal consisted of a small trailer where two men lived and worked, and a couple of air taxi outfits were there making an attempt at establishing a foothold for the big operations to come. I sometimes begged rides out to some of the remote sites with some of these pilots.

On one of these flights, in a DeHavilland Turbo Beaver, the pilot hit an unforgiving snow berm on takeoff and bent the right ski/wheel out at an ugly angle. He said to me, "How does it look over there?" I gave him the bad news. This meant an emergency landing at the Prudhoe airstrip where a couple of fire engines and an ambulance would be waiting. The pilot did a decent job of landing, holding the good gear on the ground as long as he could, balancing like a ballerina on one toe, then settling down onto the broken gear, which caved in dropping us onto the right wing, spinning us around and digging the three-bladed prop into the dirt runway bending it beyond repair. We had one passenger who was a bit wide-eyed and now had something more than living and working on the Arctic ice to write home about. I gave a written statement to the company and tried to give some credit to the pilot; however, in the back of my mind I felt like he was hotdogging it, trying to impress the folks on the ice there at the remote site by holding the plane on the ground up to the last minute before rotating up with a flurry right in front of those folks who were watching. Whoomp! When we hit the berm it knocked the breath out of me, and I thought, *Why did he do that?* The ice strip was plenty long enough, and we only had the single passenger and his gear. I think he forgot to extend his takeoff flaps.

Meanwhile, I resumed moseying about with the four-wheel drive patrol truck on what road system there was, visiting and making myself known while glassing the expanses for caribou, Arctic foxes, and snowy owls when I wasn't holed up in camp waiting for a storm to blow itself out. These storms made one sit up and take notice, the wind whipping fifty to seventy miles an hour and sometimes higher, obliterating everything and packing the crevasses of vehicles and camps with hard snow much like the consistency of sand in the desert. I understood then why the outside doors to these little camps were the same freezer doors you would ordinarily find in a meat packing plant, in this case to retain the warmth, not keep it out. You can't experience that gaping expanse along the Arctic coast, and for a hundred miles inland, without thinking of the Inupiat, who not only survived there, but thrived. It would strike you as an impossible life.

While there I investigated only one industrial fatality. In this case, a grader operator stuck in a snow bank had been mashed between his rig and a large loader as he was standing behind directing the loader to pull him out. A lonely place to die, I thought, something akin to dying in the trenches of a foreign country, maybe, and about as needless. First you are here, then you aren't.

෴

The following month was more to my liking. In May, Phil Conner, an officer from Fairbanks, and I took the state DeHavilland Beaver and a load of case gas from Fairbanks to the Junjik River in the Brooks Range, where several of us had built a plywood patrol cabin the fall before. Phil—previously a crop duster pilot from Texas—and I were on wheel/skis, which in the case of a Beaver is a heavier combination than pontoons. The day was hot as we packed the cans on snowshoes through deep snow up to the cabin where we stored them against theft by someone flying by. Leaving them out in the open would have been an invitation. By late afternoon, when we tried to take off, the snow was mushy and difficult to get on top of, though finally after several full-power runs we made it.

That's part of the reason we were low on fuel, or soon would be, after winding through the spine of the Brooks Range looking for signs of bears coming out of hibernation, and as we worked our way over to the North Slope which drains toward the Beaufort Sea. We figured on fueling at Sagwon, an oil company airstrip with some accommodations along the Sagavanirktok River, which drains into Prudhoe Bay sixty-five miles to the north. But Sagwon was fogged in, and by the time we circled around looking for a hole, it was late. We ended up landing on a frozen lake somewhere upriver from there and spent the night in the plane. Without the case gas, there was enough room to stretch out our bedrolls behind the cockpit, and it wasn't too bad.

That time of year there is quite a bit of daylight, and at some point in the early morning hours, Canada geese woke us up honking. On peeking out the portholes, we could see that they were all around the plane and were standing in puddles of water on the surface of the ice. *Water and geese?* We needed to get off this lake before it became a serious lake. Spring was here—the geese don't come north of the divide until it's very close to pairing-off and nesting time.

The DeHavilland Beaver holds 140 gallons of fuel divided between five tanks, one in each wing and three in the belly. These are only usable one at a time. In other words, you need to switch tanks manually before you run out of fuel in each, which you don't want to do, especially if low to the ground on takeoff or landing. We drained all we could out of the tanks using a five gallon can and then put all of it into a single tank. The fuel situation would be tight. We couldn't raise Sagwon on the radio from the ground so had to take off using precious fuel to gain enough altitude to call them for weather. It was marginal with some of the same fog as the night before. However, the fog had thin spots and we made it in. We felt good about that, especially since neither one of us had been to that remote site before; nor did we know where Sagwon was exactly, other than the radio signal, the location not yet showing on any sectional chart. We took on 137 gallons of fuel there, which meant we had three gallons left in an airplane that burns around twenty gallons an hour. You don't come much closer than that to hearing the silence of a dead engine, and maybe a permanent silence.

⁂

Phil and I returned to Junjik in the early fall for sheep season patrol with a Super Cub on wheels. When we landed on the sod bench above the lake, we could see that a window had been removed from the cabin and was leaning up against the side of the locked building. We thought, *Well, there went our twenty cans of fuel which we had worked so hard to carry up there and store inside.* But on closer examination the fuel was still there, though the place was a shambles from a grizzly bear visit: food cans bitten through, flour scattered and feathers from army mummy bags covering everything. Who would be so ornery as to carefully remove the entire window sash and leave the place open to the wind and rain and bears and wolverines? The evidence pointed to the bear himself. Claw marks could be seen on each side of the window opening where he had simply reached up and pulled the window loose, letting it drop in the soft tundra underneath, not even causing a pane to crack. Two men being careful with a crowbar would likely have done a messier job.

By October 23, 1970 I had the 200 flight hours necessary to be checked out in state aircraft. Phil had been helping me build those hours by letting me fly from the right seat in the Beaver, and the rear seat of a Super Cub. Phil was an instructor, so I could log hours while flying from the other seat, even though landing and taking off situated in the rear of the Cub was not an easy matter. Even at that, it had taken almost a year and a half to amass enough time, including the time I had spent flying the Cessna 180 in the

Brooks Range with Harry. Another officer, Jack Allen from McGrath, had also come over and worked with me. Jack wasn't afraid to put me in the front seat, and I was able to finally get a feel for the airplane that I needed.

Phil and I flew down to Anchorage on the big day. I took my check ride and was approved for limited flight status, meaning airport to airport only using runways of a certain length. Over time these restrictions would be lifted to allow for smaller airstrips, then off-airport landings of a certain length—gravel bars and such, then game surveys and unlimited status in a couple of years, and eventually, in later years, as a check pilot for the Department.

However, on the way back from the check ride in Anchorage, while I was flying from the front seat, we spotted a Bellanca Citabria on straight skis parked on the point of a ridge not far to the north of McKinley Park. Someone was fueling from a five gallon tin and looking up at us. Phil recognized him as Bill Hutchison, a notorious wolf poacher, who made part of his living killing wolves from the air with a shotgun, ordinarily hunting the North Slope of the Brooks Range, but occasionally suspected of hunting within McKinley National Park. We were on ski/wheels and Phil had me attempt to land in the Citabria's tracks in the deep snow while maintaining lots of power because it was uphill all the way to the top of the ridge. I didn't judge it very well and landed to the side, not maintaining power and we bogged down. We quickly dug ourselves out using snowshoes as shovels and finally made it to the top of the empty ridge where we could hear the drone of an engine fading away in the distance. The other plane had simply slipped off the steep ridge and flown away like an eagle dropping off a spruce snag and catching the wind under his wings.

Later, in Fairbanks, 'Hutch' hoorahed Phil for getting stuck while the red-faced Phil tried to explain that he had a rookie pilot in the front seat. We didn't know, of course, what Hutch had done that day, though he was the sort to brag to anyone who would listen how he couldn't be caught at his business with the wolves. In this case we never did catch him, though I wished I had the opportunity after I gained some experience and was permanently assigned to some of his favorite haunts out of Bettles Field. But that was after he had been decapitated by his own propeller in a crash up the John River in the Brooks Range.

As far as being stuck in the snow: I've been bogged down other times while on skis, but you soon learn when landing to keep up the power and stay in any tracks already there, or make a loop if the snow is more than a few inches deep, coming back into your own tracks before stopping. There is still a difference in performance, however, when you are on straight skis and alone, versus being loaded down the way Phil and I were on the ridge that day.

CHAPTER SEVEN

The Polar Bear Hunts

Guides with clients would hunt the Chukchi Sea from here all the way to the Siberian coast. These were the final years of the free-for-all killing of the big bears using airplanes.

The Fish and Game Department had only the one Super Cub at Fairbanks in 1970, which was shared with the biologists. After my check ride I didn't get the plane again until late December for a few days, again in January, then February and so on. By mid-March of '71, I had accrued about 275 total flight hours and was sent to Kotzebue with a Cub to work the polar bear hunt, a learn-as-you-go experience, believe me.

Kotzebue and the rest of the Arctic coastal area were still white that time of year—the Chukchi Sea solid and lumpy and windswept—and you couldn't tell where the land began or ended. When you topped the divide between the Koyukuk watershed and the Selawik River drainage headed toward the Arctic Circle, a white immensity of treeless, flat country greeted the eyes to the horizon and you had to trust your Automatic Direction Finder to point the way to Kotzebue on the Baldwin Peninsula 150 miles beyond. The myriad of lakes and waterways shown on the chart, and distinguishable by unique shape in the summer, were blended into a sameness, absent the trees which ordinarily outline the water in forested areas.

It wasn't until the summer of 1973, after having patrolled that country during the wintery polar bear seasons of 1971, '72, and '73, that I saw for the first time that Kotzebue and the narrow Baldwin Peninsula were in truth surrounded by the Bering Sea salt waters of Hotham Inlet and Kotzebue Sound.

At Kotzebue there were over fifty Super Cubs belonging to polar bear guides toggled to the sea ice out in front of the town. The sewage from the town of 1,500 or so people was dumped on that same ice throughout the winter to be carried away with the breakup of late spring. The danger of stepping in something was not the concern; the danger was stumbling over a frozen pile that had been dumped from a bucket, or breaking a landing gear from running into it with the airplane. Honey buckets were the order of business, and fresh-water ice was kept on the roofs of the houses and outbuildings away from the dogs and drunks. The ice was cut and hauled from the mouth of the Noatak River, the nearest source of fresh water, about fifteen miles across the sea ice on the mainland.

Guides with clients would hunt the Chukchi Sea from here all the way to the Siberian coast. These were the final years of the free-for-all killing of the big bears using airplanes. A legal hunt went like this: You would leave your home in the lower forty-eight states and fly commercially to Kotzebue or Point Hope where you would be put up in a lodge overnight. The next morning you would be buckled into the rear seat of a Super Cub and flown out on the ice to search for bears, sometimes flying over open leads of water twenty miles across. Another Super Cub with an assistant guide as a passenger would accompany you and your guide/pilot. When a bear of acceptable size was spotted, you and the assistant would be let out onto the ice; the two planes then driving the bear to you. That would be the major excitement, of course, a frightened and angry polar bear 'charging' toward you across the open ice. The bear would be killed, skinned, and the hide and skull loaded; the planes returning to Kotzebue. Jack Jonas of Jonas Brothers or some other well-known taxidermist would meet you at the tie-down and take the hide from there, usually turning it over to one of the Eskimo women to wash and flesh and prepare for shipping to Seattle or Denver for mounting. You would celebrate your good fortune that night over steak and wine, and likely return home the next day, the hunt of a lifetime over with; and the memories configured in whatever manner that made it all seem something other than it was—the bear mounted forever in a raging charge or intimidating stance, all but the slobbers frozen in perpetuity.

A charging bear was one thing; a harried bear running from an airplane into an ambush was something else and not quite so heroic if recounted with all the facts included. Admittedly, there was an element of danger involved—the largest carnivore on the continent making a beeline for you out on the open ice. It could make you feel insignificant and hopeful that the assistant guide crouched next to you was also adequately loaded for bear, and that this wasn't the first time for him too.

Although taking brown/grizzly bears the same day you were airborne was not allowed then, there was not yet a restriction of that sort for polar bears. The fair chase method of taking them without use of an airplane was almost unheard of, and normally would require the assistance of native hunters with dog teams or snow machines. One of the few guides who hunted this way was Lynn Castle, operating out of Point Barrow. Lynn later learned to fly, but was killed, stalling his own airplane into the ground while flying hunters into one of his camps on the Wood River in the Alaska Range. Lynn was an honest guide. I used him as a model of good ethics and arranged for him to teach a two-day course at the Trooper Academy. I also used him to train my stakeout officers in the art of guiding hunters, so they would better understand what went on from the guide's viewpoint. I placed these troopers, one at a time, with him during the hunting season to act as assistant guides. We licensed them as such and had them work at least two weeks guiding, packing, camp-tending, and all the rest of the hard work associated with guiding hunters.

But back to the polar bear hunts: Few, if any, of the Eskimos had airplanes; and the majority of the native hunters took pride in taking a bear using a dog team and some stalking prowess. In March of 1970, Solomon Killigvuk, an Eskimo from Point Hope, killed a large sow bear and the two young ones accompanying her. He did this the old fashioned way and without the aid of any of the guides based in Point Hope, who were themselves searching the vast ice all the way across to Siberia for signs of bear without much luck at the time. The biologist temporarily assigned there thought the two younger bears that Solomon killed were less than two years old (which defined them as cubs). This made all three of the bears illegal. No one could legally take a sow accompanied by cubs. Solomon, in this case, had taken them out on the rubbery Chukchi Sea ice alone with his dog team and was quite the talk of the village—no one having been successful in taking a bear that way for quite some time, it not being as common as you might think. However, no one, native or otherwise, was allowed to kill cubs or sows accompanied by cubs.

The biologist, John T., who was living there for the bear season with his wife and baby, had requested a wildlife officer take care of this infraction, so I was sent up there commercially all the way from where I lived in Anderson via Fairbanks, Nome, and Kotzebue. Why a pilot/officer wasn't assigned to the hunt at that time I can't say. This was before I was checked out for flight status.

By the time I got there, the hides and skulls of the three bears had been sold by Solomon to guide Don Johnson for an undisclosed amount. And even though the biologist had been ordered to seize the hides and hold them until an officer arrived, he somehow felt it unnecessary to do so, or feared the wrath of the village or the guide if he did. I seized the hides and the skulls amid some anger and contempt by the guide and the residents of the area.

At that point, the biologist got cold feet and said he wasn't sure of the ages of the young bears. Meanwhile, Solomon Killigvuk received a telegram, read to him over the BIA radio at the school, from one of the newer U.S. Senators from Alaska, Ted Stevens, congratulating him on his success as a hunter. Who put the senator up to this is anybody's guess, and it didn't matter to me, but I was having to take a closer look at all of it, not because of politics, but because the biologist was now unsure.

I took the bear hides and skulls and hopped a commercial Twin Otter flight the 150 miles south to Kotzebue the next day where two other game biologists were assigned to the hunt. But poke and prod as they did, they weren't sure either, to my disgust.

Finally, I got hold of Jerry Sexton, a polar bear specialist at Point Barrow, by telephone. (This had not been an option at Point Hope, as there were no phones there in those days—only the BIA radio at the school.) Sexton helped me identify the bears, by dental examination, as legal two-year-olds, technically no longer cubs.

I returned to Point Hope and released the hides and skulls back to Killigvuk and Johnson. I was happy about the outcome, but unfortunately, it looked to the people that politics had paid off. Regardless, I was glad to get out of there after four days of living with the biologist, John T. (whom I was miffed at for starting this whole affair without some careful biological examination of his own) and his kind wife and new baby in that cramped little one-room house with a honey bucket in the corner.

CHAPTER EIGHT

Escape from the Chandalar

*At fifty below zero, there is an ache to the still air,
something that pushes its way to the bone.*

From my Cessna 180 patrol plane, I see a lone figure standing in an easy manner out on a gravel bar of the river looking up at me. A malamute husky sits to the side and watches me in the same way, with mild curiosity. Blue cabin smoke rises out of a stand of white spruce and threads its way through the birch and across the red willows that grow here. The Middle Fork of the Chandalar River is a clear-running stream this far back into the hills. I'm tempted to land and get acquainted, as I will often do when I find someone new in this wilderness. But the Cessna is still on floats, and the river this far upstream is shallow and rocky, too much so to risk damaging the aluminum pontoons for a casual visit.

As a wildlife protection officer, this country, the Brooks Range, is eventually a part of my new assignment after arriving in Alaska. Stretched across the northern part of the state, the range lies entirely above the Arctic Circle, but it is not a desolate or treeless waste. The southern drainages of the rivers and streams are spread with white and black spruce, red willow and birch; yet, the slopes of the steep mountains are open spans of Dall sheep habitat—alpine grasses and lichens and dwarfed Arctic shrubs. The mass of the mountains themselves: the ridges, the smaller ranges within ranges, are an entangled maze you cannot see beyond. It is the definition of wilderness. From the spine of the range north, it is treeless. The north slope has a character of its own, stretching away for over a hundred miles to the Beaufort Sea coast, the whole of it horizonless white in winter, where chill factors of minus 115 degrees are experienced. Where does the land end and the sea begin?

In these first years of my assignment to the Brooks Range the Trans-Alaska Pipeline has not been built, and the country seems more whole, less violated. Now, you can crisscross it by air, admire its bulk of wild while looking down upon it; but there is a blemish, a scar: the road, the pipe—like an ugly crack on a clean windshield, one that is not repairable.

I'm posted at Bettles on the Koyukuk River, my one-man district encompassing all but the far western edges of the range. I've had to leave my wife and four children back in a small Alaskan town on the road system where there are accommodations large enough to house them along with adequate schooling. So, although this is a perfect wilderness assignment for a wildlife officer, it is lonely duty, and I will eventually seek a post which will include them.

On this September day I have been patrolling the many lakes in the upper reaches of the Chandalar watershed, checking for bear, moose and caribou hunters. In addition, since we handle police matters in our districts, it's my business to know who is new to the country.

I dip a wing in answer to the wave of the man on the gravel bar. By all appearances he is at home with his surroundings, without a care in the world. It is easy to imagine the rest of the picture, as I level out and head west: He likely has his winter meat, a moose, hung up in several sections, curing, some of it stripped for jerky. He will have most of his winter wood up, stacked in cords next to the cabin. The cabin, which is one of the four or five dilapidated log dwellings at the old gold mining settlement of Caro, has no doubt been chinked with fresh moss and otherwise readied for the coming winter, which arrives early in this Arctic country. The land here—soon to be frozen in a white shroud, where twenty below is considered comfortable—can be unforgiving to the inexperienced. I plan to check on this man's welfare in a month or so.

Some say you can't tell the difference once it gets twenty below zero or colder—thirty, forty, fifty, it's all the same. Well, that isn't true; those who have experienced it, been out in it, will agree. Certain things happen almost indiscernibly as the temperature drops. At thirty below, the cold seeps through heavy, normally warm, clothing, and the air has a crack to it; feet will begin to freeze inside winter shoepacs in thirty minutes or so. At forty below, propane freezes; and when flying you need to wear mittens inside a heated Super Cub; the snow underfoot is more brittle, like fine bits of frozen glass. At fifty below zero, there is an ache to the still air, something that pushes its way to the bone. At sixty below, it is all of the above exaggerated, nails in wooden houses popping in the night and the woods are quiet, as sensible critters lay low. At seventy below, the sap snaps in trees like rifle shots in the still woods, and splitting lake-ice booms like cannon explosions, whining as the crack reverberates at sonic speed, while otherwise it is respectfully silent everywhere. At eighty below, the air hangs heavy and will assault you when you simply open the door; and there is a tendency to pace and worry whether the house will continue to function against something akin to an infectious plague that lurks around and beyond the fragile windows, something so authoritative it has become like a living thing.

Sometime just before Thanksgiving, I make it back over to the Middle Fork. This time I am flying a smaller Piper Super Cub on skis. It is a bright day with the temperature standing around thirty below zero on the ground, not bad for this late in the year. Forty or fifty below will be the norm on a clear day in a few weeks, and in January it will occasionally dip to seventy or eighty below zero, ambient temperature. On my swing over the frozen river to check the cabin smoke for wind direction, I can plainly see snowshoed in the deep snow "H E L P" in large letters, and a larger area packed by snowshoes as a designated landing strip. The man has heard my engine from afar and has hurried out to the river, where I can see him waving frantically. I land and taxi to where he is standing and shut the engine down. His first words when I open the door are, "You got any tobacco or cigarettes?"

It is considered rude in the Alaska Bush not to be invited in for coffee or tea, especially in thirty below zero weather, but this man chooses to stand around out in the frigid air for our conversation, as if we were down by the corner drug store in June. Finally I say, "You wouldn't have any coffee at the house by chance, would you?"

"No," he says, "Not even any tea left...Say, you got any groceries or anything?"

"Sure," I say, and move around to where I can get into the baggage compartment of the airplane. "Well, not anything fancy, but I've got some freeze dried stuff here. You're welcome to some of it."

"That's great," he says, as he takes the several packages I offer.

"How come you're out of grub? Did you have a problem?"

He says he didn't accurately figure how much food they would need. They are alone, he says, just him and his new wife and their two dogs. They had been dropped off by an air taxi service out of Fort Yukon back in July, and they are not due to be picked up until sometime in April.

Already out of food? It sounds incomprehensible to me.

After I throw the cowl cover over the engine, he agrees to let me help him carry the few packages of rations up to the cabin; I am determined to take a closer look at this setup. Entering the cabin, I notice a large, young woman seated on a block of wood, facing up against, and almost eclipsing, a small wood-burning Yukon or sheepherder stove—the sort used in a tent, not for heating a big cabin. Hunched there, she methodically chucks small kindling hacked from boards into the fire, and does not particularly take notice of me as I introduce myself. Her face is dirty, her stringy hair matted, and there is a glaze in her stare. She is bundled heavily against the cold, which there is plenty of outside, but I had not expected to find it inside the cabin as well. A sheet of grinning rime ice has climbed part way up the interior walls. Open spaces between the logs are two inches wide in several places, but the worst cause of the draftiness is a large window opening which has been covered loosely with a piece of torn plastic through which their two husky dogs have free access from the outside. On the wooden table are stacked pots and pans and dishes which have not seen soap and water for some time, if ever.

One look at all this confirms my suspicions—these people are bushy. If you've ever been a little bushy, you can recognize the signs quickly: lethargy, despondency, and helplessness, with no basic comforts and routines established. You see it in their appearance, in their surroundings, and in their eyes. They need help, and sometimes they don't even know how badly they need it. I ask the young woman if she is cold. She says she hasn't been warm since early August, and here it is late November. It's not humorous at the time, but I think of Robert Service's Ballad of Sam McGee—Sam, who hadn't been warm since he "left Plumbtree, down in Tennessee."

They say they are down to eating nothing but dried peas. This, in a bountiful land. Although licensed and in possession of several weapons and some fishing gear, they haven't taken a moose or caribou, nor caught any fish in this wild country full of fish and game. They've sold their in-town possessions, he says, and invested in a stake of grub, traps, guns, how-to books, and a variety of equipment.

"I always wanted to live off the land while making a living trapping fur," he says.

But he hasn't set a trap, nor ventured more than a hundred yards from the cabin, according to what sign I could see from the air. Rather than cut down and split up the large dead spruce surrounding them, they have torn out the flooring of the old cabins for firewood. Their only exercise seems to have been the constant chucking of sticks into the little tent-stove when, within easy carrying distance, there are at least three good barrel stoves in the other cabins.

I ask if they are ready to leave.

"Yes," they are both in harmony.

Their return charter to Fort Yukon is pre-paid, he says, but he doesn't have money to get back to Fairbanks from there. He figures he will sell his guns and traps in Fort Yukon to get airfare. He offers his new .44 magnum revolver to me for a third its value, and says he'll probably have to leave his traps behind due to limited space on the chartered plane. I refuse his revolver, though I would like to have had it, but give him a fair price for the hundred or so traps and tell him to keep his guns until he gets to Fairbanks, where he can get a decent price for them. I leave the rest of my freeze dried food and tell them I'll call Fort Yukon Air Service for their charter as soon as I get back to Bettles. Within three days they are out of there.

I swing back by in a week or so while on patrol and pick up the traps. In a knapsack by the door are three frozen, feathered, undrawn grouse, which had been killed sometime over the past few months.

CHAPTER NINE

Takahula Ice

According to our agency policy, we weren't supposed to fly when the ambient temperature was colder than thirty degrees below zero. Now, I would probably listen to that advice.

Working in the bush, it's the way I arrive on the job every morning—go out and get into the airplane. In the winter it's not quite that easy: remove the cowl cover, remove the catalytic heater from under the cowling, sweep the snow off the wing and tail surfaces, take off the wing covers, remove the wooden blocks from under the skis (the skis are elevated each night to prevent their sticking to the snow), untie the airplane (embarrassing if you forget to untie the tail), and then do your normal pre-flight.

The cockpit of the Super Cub doesn't warm up right away; you best be dressed for the elements. It won't get warm until after takeoff, and maybe not even then if it's forty below zero or so. But, I would want to be dressed warmly anyway, and hold the temperature low inside the airplane to keep from becoming damp from perspiration. What I have on my back might be all I get out with from a burning or wrecked Cub. For that reason, I strap my emergency pack and snowshoes to the wing struts on the Cub.

One winter I had a frozen battery on the Cub all season, so ended up hand-propping everywhere I went: magnetos off and throttle back, mixture full lean, then swing prop through a few times to lubricate the pistons, position prop at proper angle, mixture full rich, two shots of prime, crack throttle a half inch, mags on, swing prop counterclockwise (should fire after two or three tries—maybe the first try). If it doesn't fire, it's probably flooded. Mags off, mixture full lean, throttle full on, reverse prop through several times (fuel will be dripping out of the carburetor; a backfire while propping may cause a fire in the carburetor now, in which case the start-up will need to be made immediately to suck out the fire—*hustle, hustle*—or forfeit the airplane if you don't have a fire extinguisher), repeat earlier starting procedure without priming (mustn't forget to decrease the throttle; this is where they chew you up and fly away without you).

Sometimes the ice you're standing on can be tricky. The safest way I found to prop a Piper Super Cub is from behind the prop: one-handed, single mag on to lessen the compression, left hand gripping door opening for stability, right-hand propping. Safe. Well, safer. I don't always feel safe around flying machines. Maybe most of us don't, which is probably the healthiest position. A person needs to be thinking clearly in and around them. Like a free-spirited mule, they might kick you when you least expect it if you become too sure of yourself or too complacent.

Cold is cold anywhere you are. Defining just how cold in terms of human discomfort varies from place to place. My mother complained of being cold in Albuquerque when it dropped to fifty degrees—quite pleasant to someone recently from the grips of an Arctic winter. Even in the Arctic it varies considerably to individual tastes, shall we say, or hardships. Ron McClellan, a physician's assistant of several years in the Arctic and elsewhere, says the most cases of hypothermia he ever witnessed were in the San Diego, California area, and the most cases of heat exhaustion were along the Beaufort Sea coast of Alaska in the winter, both caused by not preparing properly for weather or conditions—the over-dressed Arctic workers working up a sweat. Exposure means everything, I guess, or the lack of it.

༄

According to our agency policy, we weren't supposed to fly when the ambient temperature was colder than thirty degrees below zero. That was the written policy, and probably a good one, all things considered. Now, I would probably listen to that advice and abide by it. Somewhere along the line, I suppose, we develop wisdom.

However, while assigned to Bettles Field, north of the Arctic Circle, most of the good flying days in the winter are in the fifty below zero range. These are blue and white bright days, the slanted sun giving definition to signs along the snow. The only clouds are clouds of steam coming off a few open stretches of river water, or ice fog surrounding the bush settlements with wood stoves billowing frosted vapor you can see for miles.

The poachers don't observe our thirty-below policy, and the only days of sunshine—the sun affords the best tracking conditions—are those off-limit, cold ones. If you wait till the weather warms up to fly, you might as well park until spring...late spring. If the weather warms up to legal flying temperature before spring, it means cloud cover and snow with gray days, poor visibility, and warm melting winds—the chinooks. You don't mind flying on those days, but for tracking you need sun for definition-shadowing and contrasting lines across the snow. In addition, you can easily locate any camps or cabins, which may be overlooked at other times of the year, as the frozen smoke lifts out above the trees and shines like a signal beacon in the cold air, the crystal smoke so white the snow often looks gray in comparison.

The winter days are short enough in the Arctic without wasting them sitting on the ground. At best, you might get two or three hours of daylight in December if it's not overcast.

So, I chose to ignore the cold weather rule to make myself useful. (Rules are made in offices somewhere, don't you know?) The truth of all the danger lies somewhere in the middle, actually. I do a lot of flying at fifty below zero and colder—climb up and catch the inversion where the temperature is twenty or so degrees warmer and go on about my way. But the failure of machines happens down in the pits of the cold, at those critical times: the landings and takeoffs.

Case in point:

I land at Takahula Lake on the raw ice where someone is staying at the Helmricks cabin. It's a part of the job to make safety checks on folks in the backcountry, especially in winter. There's no snow on the lake itself; the winds have blown it clear and clean. It shines, like burnished steel, and depending on the angle of attack, the ice can be blue, gray, white, slate, black, and even pink, the shades defying standard terms we've invented for colors. It's sixty below zero here. The white vapor from the little cabin's wood stove lies low to the ground on this windless day, creating a mist of ice-fog. All the frosted, frozen things—from axe handles to door handles to spruce trees—are hoary with the rime of it.

This Cessna 180 I'm flying for part of the winter while assigned to Bettles doesn't like the cold. It belches and coughs on takeoff at fifty below—you need to keep carburetor heat on until you're rolling with full power, then ease it off. The Super Cub with its Lycoming engine is more tolerant of the bitter cold than the Continental engine of the 180.

I land on the stiff ice at Takahula. Like metal to metal, the skis rattle and bang. If I'd been more sensible, I would have left the skis retracted and landed on wheels. Then again, if I had more sense I'd have stayed at the house in Bettles. There isn't any stopping short on this stuff, especially on skis—no brakes. You would swear the airplane speeds up when you relax the weight of the airplane onto the ice while on skis. The landing is smooth enough; it's the run-out down the lake that's rough. *Rattley-bang.* A cable to the toe of my left ski snaps, flying back, slapping the plexiglass windscreen to where I think it should shatter.

I don't know how an airplane keeps from falling to pieces at these temperatures—the metal, the rubber, the plastic is so brittle and vulnerable to breaking. (Once, when I got in my patrol vehicle on a seventy-four below zero morning—I remember the incident, but not why it was so urgent to be driving on that day—the floor mats shattered under my feet like thinly-made peanut brittle, and the rubber molding around the door splintered away like crystal glass when I slammed the door.)

So, why would anyone want to chance it? Why bend an airplane when everything around you is waiting to kill you without really wanting to? There is no malice here; it's just a respect the Arctic demands. There's no forgiveness. Death is just a part of life. *Chance* is often what everything does or does not survive by: chance that a moose is in the path of a hunting wolf pack; chance that the ice covered by snow over the swift channel of a river might be crossed by an unsuspecting soul at the very spot it is the thinnest, and the gurgling water gulps him up; chance that a chimney fire consumes a cabin and its inhabitants; chance that a pilot busts his airplane and dies of exposure, maybe, because no other fools are out risking their valued equipment and valued butts in this inhospitable chill to chance by and see him there. But, just by chance, he happens to land at an inhabited lake in a land of uninhabited lakes, and there is someone there with the tools to fix his indiscretions. And back at Bettles on flare-out, just the back pressure on the controls is enough to snap them off in his hand. Quickly grabbing the control column post is all that saves him from dumping the airplane. The leaf-hopping down the runway while trying to salvage the landing only creates an embarrassment, and then only if someone is watching—but, of course, someone is always watching a bad landing.

CHAPTER TEN

The Wolfers

Wolves do not mistake the sound of the Piper Super Cub; those ignoring it do not live long.

Athabascan trapper, Edmund Lord, has noticed that someone else is sharing his trapline area with him. On one of his rounds while checking his line, he sees airplane ski tracks and footprints leading to an unusual trap-set, something he hasn't seen before. When he brushes away some of the small pieces of caribou meat surrounding the set, an explosion sends him reeling backward into the snow. He sits there in a stupor, staring back at the device that has violated the winter silence, scaring the hell out of him there on the frozen river, eighty miles from the nearest habitation. He gathers his wits and begins to examine himself for injuries. His right glove is torn by the blast, but his hand is not injured.

Edmund is lucky. The blast is from a cyanide gun, referred to commonly as a "coyote getter" in the West. If the powdered cyanide had entered his bloodstream through an open cut, he would have died. If he had breathed the vapor expelled from the blast, it would have paralyzed his lungs immediately. In six seconds an adult coyote can run a hundred yards. That's as far from a cyanide gun as I ever found one after he had gasped the exploding powder, when I used them in my work while controlling predators in New Mexico. In other words, as far as the coyote could get with air no longer being a factor in his life. That is how quickly Edmund would have died: a few seconds—not even enough time to reach his snowmachine seventy-five feet away.

But Edmund did not know what it was that blew up in front of him, even after he dug the gun out of the frozen ground and studied it. It was in a small metal tube, driven into the ground, and there was a trigger mechanism screwed onto a wax-coated, hollow, cloth-covered barrel an inch long, smeared with caribou blood. Inside was a spent .38 caliber pistol cartridge. He knew then that it was some kind of set gun, but who the hell would be using .38 caliber set guns on his trapline? He gathered up his rifle, stuffed the coyote getter in his coat pocket, and headed for home. He sent word to me when he got there.

As soon as he shows me the getter, I know what it is. They were an effective way of thinning out the coyotes in New Mexico, before they were outlawed for predator control. In Alaska they are definitely illegal to use for taking wolves or anything else.

Edmund is already upset over someone moving in on his trapline. When I tell him how close he came to having more than just a bullet through the hand, he becomes angry. "I want this person caught," he says, "One of my kids could've been with me, and maybe this damned thing would've killed him."

He says he has noticed a red airplane in the area, but never close enough to see the numbers. He says he found once, by their tracks, where they had killed a wolf, not by trapping, but by shooting. At least he thought it was by shooting. When he examined the site where the two people had picked up the wolf along the frozen river, there was no blood, nor sign of blood in the wolf tracks, yet the wolf had been running hard when he died. If he had backtracked the wolf, he would have found a discharged cyanide gun.

Edmund flies out to the scene with me to examine the place where the wolf had been taken. The tracks lead back to the river bank, where, by sign of the birds and a disturbed area in the snow, along with bits of meat and suet, there appears to have been a getter set. Closer examination produces a cyanide gun. It has been discharged, but not reset.

"Do you know who might own the red plane you saw?" I ask Edmund. He names a local big-game guide. I then recall that this guide indeed has a red Super Cub. Things begin to come together. I had received a call only two days before from a friend of the guide who said he had a wolf to bounty. This would be our wolf.

After dropping Edmund off, I stop by to bounty the wolf. At that time the State is paying a fifty-dollar bounty on wolves. The man leads me around to a shed where he pulls out the hide of a large gray wolf. There is a yellowish residue surrounding the area of the mouth—a familiar sight to me. Dried saliva mixed with cyanide powder.

I ask him where the carcass is. He says they burned it yesterday in the trash dump, so it "wouldn't attract animals."

He says he wants to bounty the wolf for the guide, who has actually taken the animal. He says the guide is not there, but another fellow is there who was with the guide when they took it. I take the hide and go to see him. After questioning, he admits they have taken the wolf with a cyanide gun. He says he brought the guns up from Wyoming where he has a friend who gave them to him. He gives me the rest of the guns, about a dozen.

I have the hide examined at the State Trooper crime lab. The residue is cyanide. I have my case.

But not so fast—there's a technicality. The court rules that the law has been "improperly promulgated." Therefore, it has not actually been in effect. Sometimes it pays to hire a high-powered, defense attorney.

⁓

When I talked to the naturalist at McKinley Park, Dr. Adolph Murie, about the wolf case, he said he hadn't heard of cyanide guns being used in Alaska since the early fifties when the federal government was trying to eradicate the wolves. Now, he said he felt the greatest detriment to the wolf was the use of the airplane by hunters and trappers as a weapon. I soon had to agree.

The sound of a Piper Super Cub has a significant meaning to a wolf— that particular engine chatter differentiated from the drone of any other fixed-wing aircraft or the whopping of a helicopter—the Super Cub signifying death advancing from the sky, like some monstrous mechanical eagle spitting fire and lead bullets. Wolves do not mistake the sound of the Super Cub, the most common airplane used by wolf killers; those ignoring it do not live long.

The age-old castigation of the "evil" gray wolf had reached the height of effectiveness at this time. The market value for a wolf hide was high, and Alaska was still forking out fifty bucks in bounty. Trapping was not the most efficient way to decimate the population. Practically every pilot with a rag airplane and a shotgun was in the air after wolves. Propellers were shot off, struts were shot off, but the war was on, and hundreds of pellet-ridden wolf hides were being bid on by the fur buyers. Yet, these were legal hides, for the most part.

A few bucks bought a trapper's license which entitled the "trapper" to take ten wolves by shotgunning from an airplane in most game management units. Our job trying to enforce that limit was impossible. The north slope of the Brooks Range, lying across the entire breadth of the State—a treeless landscape of rolling hills and measureless plains—was plucked practically clean of Arctic grays.

If you are a wolf on the treeless tundra, you do not hide under a dwarf birch; you cannot hide, so you run. And you stop running only when you are dead, or when you lie down in the snow exhausted, awaiting your fate. Or, if you are fortunate, you stop when the giant bird has run out of ammo or is short of fuel and finally leaves.

Hutchinson, the lone outlaw wolf hunter I mentioned earlier, would take several hundred a year from the Arctic country. He bragged about killing entire packs on a single foray, holding the controls between his knees and firing the shotgun out of the side door. He passed the word that we weren't talented enough to catch him. Maybe not. When we found his decapitated body in his broken airplane on the John River in the Brooks Range, and after shotguns had been banned for taking wolves in any manner, the shotgun cartridges picked up at the wreckage were hand-loaded with small caliber rifle slugs rather than pellets. The chase is a compelling thing.

Not all wolves run from people. During the building of the Trans-Alaska Pipeline, not too far from Toolik construction camp, a female gray wolf developed a system of stopping trucks along the Haul Road. She had learned where the sandwiches came from—the ham on rye, peanut butter and jelly, cold beef and mustard. Her plan was simple: lie in the middle of the road awaiting the arrival of an eighteen-wheeler, shocking the driver into stopping; advance then to the driver's side and stand by for the forthcoming handout. Later, in the summer, after her pups were whelped, she was often seen lying in the road, her pups obediently sitting at the shoulder of the road watching, learning the ropes.

Fourteen years later, I am traveling by pick-up through that Arctic area north of the Brooks Range, and am not surprised to see, fifteen miles north of Toolik Lake, a medium-sized wolf sitting along the road waiting for me to get there. *What generation is she?* I wonder, as I pull up alongside her. *Does she have a den full of pups over there toward the river?* I shut the engine off and just sit there talking to her as she looks at me uninterested, occasionally snapping her jaws at an offending mosquito circling her head, but seldom taking her eyes off mine. I finally give up the waiting game and drive on. She remains there, waiting for an easier touch.

I was plagued by the incident. I wondered if we really wanted the wild wolf becoming complacent in the presence of man, losing a well-earned fear, and if we wanted wildlife to be hooked on leftovers, handouts, and garbage. Or maybe I simply didn't recognize a "natural" course of events. After all, man and his leftovers are a natural part of things, too. Did I always want wolves to flee when I met them in the wild, or is it a fortunate event to spend a few reflective moments, eyeball to eyeball, thought to thought, with a ferine gray wolf in its natural habitat and with the freedom to leave? And I further wondered, should we continue to accord unto ourselves the right to decide the ultimate fate of the North American gray wolf?

The wolf deserves better than all the hoopla which has been building to a crescendo for the last fifty years or more. My admiration for the wolf didn't vanish, but in some ways, I was fearful of being tagged as belonging to one radical side or the other. Without having studied the phenomena of why society polarizes itself on every issue, I'm amazed nevertheless: exalted-wolf-of-mystic-qualities lovers to the left, scorned-wolf-of-game-killing-gluttony haters on the right.

The aboriginal Alaskan, who generally keeps outside most of this, must be in awe of the argument—he knowing the value of the wolf simply for what he is: both a hungry killer of things to eat and a spiritual animal of power. The wolf himself would, no doubt, be in awe of even that description. If blessed with reasoning, he would vow contentment in simply being a wolf, happy to be left alone to his own devices.

I spent twenty-five years or so snooping in and around the wolf's haunts mostly as a hunter, a guide, a game warden, and later, just an observer. I seldom saw him in the rough except while tracking him from the air in the winter, finding his predatory kills and landing there to check the remains and extract a sample of bone marrow for research to determine health condition of the moose or caribou prior to death. It was at those times I learned a little about his killing nature, enough to respect the power of jaws capable of breaking open the femur bone of an adult moose, enough to know a hungry pack utilized what they killed—hide, bones, viscera, meat—all down to just a few big, broken bones left half-drained of marrow, and bits of tallow scattered for the ravens and gray jays to pick at.

Although I camped out in wolf country often, it wasn't often I'd hear a wolf. The first was in the fall of my third year in Alaska, about sixty miles up the Nixon Fork of the Takotna River. I was camped in a tent on a gravel bar with my three young sons, lying in my bedroll listening to the drone of an elusive mosquito, when I heard a wolf howl in the distance—a hollow sound, muted by the fog, coming out of the dim light of late night. It signified to me the truest form of wildness and wilderness. Not just because Aldo Leopold said so, but because I felt it myself, and it was like there was a truth out there I could almost reach out and touch. The wolf's ordinarily unfettered presence meant something more than a photo, or a china etching, a carved fetish, or a Paul Winters tape; more than a road-side zoo of chained-up hybrids or a pack of wild wolves running from an airplane. It certainly was something more than howl-ins on the sidewalks of LA or fist-clenching in-the-name-of-science squabbles at the game board meetings in Alaska.

In my life I've run the gamut of wanting to kill wolves in defense of what man determines are his rightful possessions, to a personal truce, exalting him to some level of spirituality. But somewhere in the recent past I reverted to thinking of him as I originally did that night on the Nixon Fork over forty years ago: as an animal living his life in the wilderness, and living it best, it seems to me, without too much attention by man.

CHAPTER ELEVEN

Lake of Grace

You don't walk through a stopped airplane propeller, period, unless you don't care whether you live or die.

The Meador family had been in the headwaters of the Wild River of the Brooks Range for twelve years by 1969, if I recall correctly, and it may well be that their young son, Dion, had never been out of the Arctic wilderness. I first met them that fall in the Brooks while working with the biologist/pilot Harry. Wildlife Officer Buck Masters had dropped by Bettles to pick me up this day.

Masters was a no-nonsense talker, meaning he said what was on his mind—not an advantageous sort to have with you sometimes. He was a crafty enough bush officer, but it was possible to be crafty without being obscene, and Masters could be obscene with regularity.

At the Meadors' place on Wild Lake, Masters was like a coot strayed from the water. His abrupt manner scraped like a rasp over that reticent family's quiet style of living, even though he wanted to leave the impression of feeling at ease when he wasn't. He just didn't approve—I suppose that's what it was—of their back-to-nature style of living, and he told me he figured they were the original hippies, meaning something derogatory, I could sense. They, who dined with hand-carved eating utensils, lived on a dirt floor, read books more common to back-East intellectuals than western game wardens, and wore home-spun clothes.

Fred Meador—the locals had re-named Wild Lake to "Wildman Lake" to honor him—was a photographer of accomplishment, some of his work having been contracted and sold to Walt Disney Studios. The "wildman" idea must have come from his manner of living, rather than his demeanor, as I found him to be polite, bright, friendly, and talkative—a thin man in a heavy country.

At the supper table, Officer Masters was asked to say grace. He didn't hesitate a moment: "Rub-a-dub-dub, pass the grub, yea, yea, yea, Jesus," he said, and reached for the platter of meat and potatoes. The Meadors looked at one another, at Masters, at me, but had the good grace not to say anything. It was interesting to flush the real barbarian here.

Fred had been making his own film documentary on their year-round life in the Arctic wilderness. It perplexes me that on the final trip, an outside junket to San Francisco to put the finishing touches on his film, he walked into the propeller of the Cessna 185 float plane he had chartered to take him from his wilderness homestead to the village of Bettles Field. To me, the accident was unbelievable; Fred Meador had been around float planes for over seventeen years by then and knew the safe protocol around flying machines better than most.

When Fred and his charter pilot taxied up to the floating dock along the Koyukuk River at Bettles Field, he hopped out onto the passenger-side float to secure the plane. This was common practice, and one the pilot is comfortable with if the passenger is experienced with the procedure, which Fred surely had to have been. Docking on the passenger side, even while alone, a pilot can coordinate his taxi/tie-down to coincide with the easing up to the dock against the current: He chops the power by starving the engine of fuel with the mixture control, cuts the mags, slides to the passenger side, and climbs out in time to intercept the dock as the float slides up to it. The line, tied to the toe cleat of each float and trailing back almost to the water rudders, is picked up, and as he steps to the dock, he is ready to secure the plane. Having a passenger familiar with the routine, and willing to perform it, can be an advantage.

There are rules though. While on the pontoon one never walks forward of the wing strut of a Cessna while approaching the dock; the engine compression sometimes causes the stopping prop to suddenly reverse, like a rubber band unwinding. In fact, you don't walk through a stopped prop, period—it's taboo, like not standing in front of the muzzle of a gun (not knowing if it is loaded or not), unless you don't care if you live or die. When a pilot has passengers unfamiliar with docking procedures, he can still safely handle the docking by himself with a little practice: hopping out of his own door and crawling across the pontoons' spreader bar under the fuselage, requiring a certain agility. But even then, he never strays forward of the wing strut on a Cessna.

At any rate, Fred Meador stepped out of the passenger's side, took hold of the trailing line, clambered forward of the wing strut—for who knows why—and walked right into the prop, which was still spinning a blurred circle as they approached the dock. Was his mind already somewhere in San Francisco?

Or was it still preoccupied with another tragedy?

Not long before, Fred and his wife had gone outside to spend some time working on the editing of the film, leaving their son alone at the lake. The boy was by then about seventeen, certainly comfortable in the wilderness if anyone ever was. There was an old handmade canoe the boy frequently used to paddle around the lake. Wild Lake is large, almost a mile wide, maybe, by three or four long.

On the day of this tragedy, the old canoe turned over on him out in the middle, and he was hanging on to it, shouting in the wilderness for someone to help. The only other soul around was a young squatter by the name of Alleman spending the fall in a cabin down the lake. He heard Dion, and from the shore yelled encouragement as he hurriedly searched about for a log or something to float out with, but to his anguish there was nothing. After a long while the boy went under. Alleman said Dion never panicked, that he seemed to patiently hold on as long as he could while Alleman searched the shore for something to use, yelling out that he was coming, he was coming.

It was late fall in the Brooks Range, within a few days of ice forming, when air and water transportation cease to exist. Yet, it likely would be weeks before the ice thickened enough to support an airplane. Alleman sat down and wrote a letter to Dion's parents, Fred and Elaine, describing what had happened. It was a month or more before it could be mailed, and before anyone else even knew of the drowning. All the Meadors could do when they returned was to look across the snow and ice, and hope to recover the body in the spring. But the lake had digested young Dion. The cold, deep-water lakes of Alaska often do not give up their dead.

Fred blamed himself for not being there when his son drowned.

When Fred stepped through the floatplane propeller, the pilot blamed himself for *being* there—being there and allowing Fred to go forward of the strut without somehow stopping him. Possibly, it haunts him still. I hope not.

Be that as it may, the last time I landed there nobody lived at the Meador place on the upper end of Wild Lake. It was brambles and fireweed and old uncared-for logs; the salty handles of old tools chewed by porcupines and mice. The blueberry and low-bush cranberry shrubs and lichens had reclaimed the long-ago used water-bucket trail down to the shore. It was the sort of place you run across back in the hills somewhere and think, *I wonder what the story was here?*

PART THREE: THE RIVER COUNTRY

"...What good heed Nature forms in us!
She pardons no mistakes.
Her yea is yea, and her nay, nay."
— Ralph Waldo Emerson

CHAPTER TWELVE

Among the River People

They saw a dead horse along the river bank, and Carl asked his father what sort of animal it was. His father said it was a "white man's dog."

McGrath is a big village on a bend of the muddy Kuskokwim River, across from where the clearwater Takotna flows in. It is a busy village, centered around its primary industry, flying, with the main street part of the airport taxiway. We get settled in, my family and I. Once again, the woods butt up against town and provide a playground for the kids. A twenty foot riverboat suffices for Sunday drives and picnic excursions. In the summer and winter I often park the patrol plane on the river, which fronts the two-story log house we live in. There are no roads that lead out of this country. The nearest city is Anchorage, over 200 miles across the Alaska Range by air. My one-man district is the size of Oregon and includes several mountain ranges, all of the Kuskokwim River and its watershed, and the lower 400 miles or so of the Yukon River.

I'm the only law enforcement officer for McGrath and several surrounding villages. There is no one else to shove the dirty work off to. Even though we Fish and Game officers have not yet been transferred to the State Troopers, we are still expected to perform as peace officers. In Alaska at this time there are not enough police officers to cover the bush country, and we game wardens are the only pilot/officers throughout the entire state.

A little after midnight the phone rings. I get out of bed, go downstairs to answer it. "There's a drunk down here at the bar...causin' trouble...won't leave."

"Which bar?"

"McGuire's. Keeps pickin' fights."

"Tell him to go home. Tell him if he doesn't, I'll be down to arrest him."

There are no arguments here with city, borough, state or federal officers about who will handle what. There isn't anyone else; I will handle it, whatever it is. And there are no back-ups; that stuff is only in the cities.

At 1:30 A.M., the phone rings, "There's a fight down here at McGuire's Tavern."

"I'll be right there."

Get dressed, bundle up, walk the frozen snow (*crunch, crunch*) down to the bar. The old beater 'patrol' truck is buried under four feet of hard-packed snow, and it's too cold at 40 below to get the snowmachine started. Hope the fight's over before you get there. There's no jail this side of Anchorage. If you arrest someone, you put them out in the tool shed, handcuff them to a support bar, light the stove, hire a citizen as a jail guard to make sure they don't get hurt or, at forty or fifty below, the stove doesn't go out. Take them to the magistrate the next morning, and maybe a commercial flight to Anchorage if they get jail time. But at McGuire's the fighting's over, the fighters are gone; broken pool cue, a little blood. We'll see if someone wants to file a complaint in the morning.

Break-ins, assaults, deaths, drunks, bar fights, family squabbles, property damage, child abuse, drugs, search and rescues, rapes—there's no escape. If you're off in some distant range of the district investigating something else, you have not dodged it; it will be there when you get back. This is in the days before we have constables and village police officers in the bush.

༄

There's banging on the door at 3 A.M. "My neighbor busted out my porch light. Said it was botherin' him!"

"Here's a quarter. Go buy another one. Don't come over here waking me up for this kind of bullshit."

༄

The previous wildlife officer assigned here, Jack Allen, said he got tired of answering the door in the wee hours. He let them bang away, and if they didn't leave after a while, he answered it. One twilight morning at four, he hears banging at the door. The banger leaves a little past the cut-off point. Jack thinks, *What the hell, maybe it's important*; goes downstairs, opens the door. A guy is walking off down the road. "Whatta ya want?" Jack shouts.

"Thought you might want to know your airplane's floatin' down the river."

That gets Jack's attention. Running out to the river in his underwear, he can just see the floatplane disappearing around a far bend. He grabs the river boat and gives chase—some crazy guy in his underwear out on the river. He is lucky the little Super Cub hasn't dug a wing into the bank, hit the barge tied up just downriver, or hit a sweeper. Chugging back up the river towing the boat behind, swatting mosquitoes off bare legs, he thinks, *Someday I could write a book about all this, but would have to call it fiction.*

In the summer I have to leave McGrath and the upper villages to handle their own problems. Most of my days now are spent on the lower Kuskokwim and Yukon rivers patrolling the commercial salmon fisheries by air—hundreds of small one- and two-man skiffs drifting for king salmon with seven or eight fishing districts opening and closing at different times. I use the old Cessna 180 on floats (the only one the Department owns at that time), flying eight and ten hours a day, fueling from five-gallon tins purchased in the river villages, eating out of a paper sack, sleeping sometimes in the plane while tied to the river bank or on a quiet lake somewhere, or sometimes in a shack or tent. When it works out, I occasionally stay overnight at the St. Mary's Catholic Mission on the Andreafsky River, just off the Yukon. Good food, thoughtful people.

The nuns at St. Mary's would think it scandalous not to be dressed in habit, and they look better that way anyway; they are more streamlined and dignified. Most of them are old nuns—over eighty, over ninety—looking somewhat swallowed up, but lovely in their sanctity. I bring them fresh Yukon king salmon, and they are happy, these old sisters—living there in the lower villages since the days when they were bright-eyed girls fresh out of a faraway place.

I was at St. Mary's Mission when the pope died—we heard the news on the radio—but I noticed no more reaction than if I were among Baptists down at the drugstore on Main Street, USA; though maybe I'm not Catholic enough to understand. But the day seemed ordinary, like maybe the pope had moved to St. Louis, Missouri or something.

༄

Throughout this country the Yukon is wide, often more than a mile. And when you fly, you see distinct bluffs from afar and know the river lies there, the bluffs and hills always north of the river. And from one bluff to another may be twenty or thirty miles across the flats, with the river wandering where it wants to, but always meeting you again at the next bluff. And then beyond, there's another bluff....

Enter, in the heat of midday, Holy Cross, a large Athabascan village, silent to the last dog, and know that the people and the dogs must be dead—there has been a report of someone with a gun threatening everyone. But no, that someone is sleeping it off; it is simply midday. Midnight will be different, a time to live, time to fire up a tune on the guitar or a three-wheeler. Kids play and shout all night out in the streets. Booze in town (a flight came in today from Bethel). *Here's to you as good as you are; weep me a tune on the gitfiddle of broken strings.*

Gang-bang rape, they tell me; victim drunk too. She says they all did it to her, even the old man, ninety-two. "Yes, I think he did, I think he did!" The old man says, "Hell, if I'd of done it, she'd know for sure!" She weeps with drunken eyes. Is there a real world somewhere? Sure, you're standing in it. That booze no goddamn good for this place!

Young guys stole a three-wheeler from the Catholic priest, Father Mike. He didn't radio for the cops to fly in; he found out who did it—kicked some butt. They didn't do it again.

Out on the river, the fish wheels thrum in ceaseless, ancient currents, now and then snatching a silver fish, threading it flopping into the catch box. Fish wheels: the chirp of heavy wood on heavy wood.

༄

Sometimes I stay at the site of an abandoned village near the big bend of the Yukon, back behind the bluffs. It is called Ohogamiut, a place no longer a place. In the high grass against the hill, a frayed Russian Orthodox church stands. Here, the site of an old village under the grass somewhere. One old cabin is still there below the church, standing with four walls and a partial roof; and if you lack shelter, it is a good place, but airy and damp, with bugs in thunderous herds. The smoldering Buhach powder helps thin them out.

You could stay in the unlocked church, I suppose. There is a small bell there cast in honor of that place and dated seventeen something, and old Russian books, and all the trappings—the whole of it needing, in some musty pleasure, to be alone. But you wouldn't be comfortable there. You wouldn't want to smoke or spit or pass gas. You would stay instead in the fallen-down log place where Old Glory is rolled on its staff, leaning in a dry corner. It is a manufactured flag, thirteen stars in a circle, but in a different configuration than the one Betsy Ross designed. Old. When I see the flag, I leave it there, but I'm sorry later. I think, *Why didn't I take that flag?* Eight years later I'm flying on floats in that area and make a special stop. The roof has fallen in on the old cabin, but against the wall, protected by fallen timbers, the flag is still there. I am happy about that.

I take a few pictures, and I leave it once again.

☙

Here, in much of this Oregon-sized district where I work, there is no one else to check on the welfare of lone residents, those who are divorced from the villages, who prefer the solitude and independence of living away from some of the strife. Sometimes I pick up the mail for whomever lives along my planned route of patrol, or pick up a needed mechanical part for someone. Old Deacon Deaphon tells me, over coffee at his cabin above Devil's Elbow on the Kuskokwim, "This radio don't talk no more." I have it fixed for him the next time I am in town.

Occasionally I bring some fresh fruit to Deacon and Agnes, who goes about the household chores in a homemade wheel chair. "We glad like hell you come!" she says. There is a pleasure in the voice. They are Athabascans, he in his eighties, she probably ten years younger. I'm told Agnes is one of the last to know the art of making fish nets from animal sinew. She says she is the daughter of "Nushagak Man," whom she never saw—he died back in the '30s—but whom she knew to be the wild man who roamed the mountains of the upper Holitna and Nushagak watersheds in the old days.

Old Deacon, although elderly and sore-footed, stands straight. He is several inches taller than the average Athabascan and is barrel-chested. He does not live near any of the villages and is, I believe, a free spirit, living solely off the land and with dignity while doing so. He and Agnes raised several children. Most of them lived to adulthood, with all but one daughter dying violent deaths up and down the river. They are buried there on the hill behind the house, those that the river or a fire have given up.

When their last surviving and youngest son, an adult of thirty-some by then, was killed in a local snowmachine accident, the river was breaking up and running heavy ice; I couldn't land to tell them, so I dropped a note explaining the circumstances. Fortunately, an older grandchild was there who could read. I asked them to meet the plane at a large snow-covered gravel bar upriver the next day, for delivery of the body. Some weeks later a Deaphon granddaughter stopped by my office in McGrath and presented me with a gift from her grandparents. It was a child's fur marten hat, carefully made and addressed to my youngest son.

One fall before I knew him, Deacon shot and killed his son-in-law. They were hunting moose together, and Deacon said he thought the man was a black bear. It was well known that the son-in-law was a worthless, wife-beating, child-abusing drunk. Deacon had spent his entire life in the wilds. It is my opinion that on that particular day, the hunting season was open for worthless sons-in-law.

༄

Most of the settlers and life-long residents I met in the back country had what you might call a free spirit. And most had stories of interest in their past, whether it was Sam Wright, who had taken a sabbatical from his professorship of theology at Stanford to follow Bob Marshall's trail through the Brooks Range, liked what he saw, and never went back to his students—or eighty-five-year-old Carl Susui, an Athabascan from the village of Telida, who saw the first white man to enter the upper Kuskokwim country.

A few years before he died, Carl, who was the son of an old Athabascan chief, told me about those first white men. They were soldiers on an expedition into the interior from the sea, before the turn of the century. He said that he and his father were in a canoe one day in late fall, hunting moose downstream from the tiny village. They saw a dead horse along the river bank, and Carl asked his father what sort of animal it was. His father said it was a "white man's dog." They killed a black bear the next day near that area, and its stomach contained a large amount of bacon, yet undigested. They backtracked the bear for most of the day to see where the bacon had come from and finally trailed it into the soldiers' camp.

Carl said the weather had been turning cold, with some snow on the ground, and that the eight white men found in camp were suffering and appeared lost. He and his father led them to the village where they stayed the winter. His mother made them parkas, mittens, and moosehide boots. In the spring, his father led the men across the hills to Lake Minchumina and showed them the trail that would take them to Fort Gibbon (now the village of Tanana) on the Yukon River. Carl said his family never received any recognition from the government for their help.

~

Down on the lower Yukon River, the delta villages lie split along the mud banks. The houses all face the river channel, which cuts through the center of the villages like a thoroughfare—U.S. Highway 160 through Cherokee, Kansas, maybe, although the flatness, and the sameness, and the grayness isn't broken by section-line county roads or wire fence rows. Here, with dirty glass windows, the houses sit unblinking, as though wide-eyed in curiosity, watching the brown water move thickly on its way to a pallid sea, a sea that hides somewhere to the west, the river having to feel its way with probing fingers to find it.

You could not find the sea yourself without knowing the channels by instinct, because as far as you can see, on a clear day even, there are only thin, flat, ruled lines of horizon where near meets far in a sameness, a grayness, a flatness. And though much of this broad, muddy delta is called land, and some think they might own it, there are great masses under water at high tide; and out where sea and river become one or the other, there is only brown water, and maybe you can see a camp on stilts just poked up in the middle of nowhere, with some guy sitting on the steps drinking a beer.

The villages, with their trash-covered banks, straddle the sloughs which are veins of the big river and serve as off-ramps from the watery Yukon freeway for the flat-bottomed skiffs and floatplanes. No one seems to care that the banks are loaded with boat hulls, sunken houses, wringer washers, kicker motors, oil drums, trash heaps, and dog carcasses. What the hell, the junk might help stop the erosion, you see; and out here you want to stop the natural erosion because if you don't, the grinding river will carry you and your possessions off into the Bering Sea.

Here, the wind does not know east from west, but blows around the compass, one way or another, always, and you are glad it does in the summer, because the bugs would kill you if it didn't. But in the winter: Why does the wind have to blow in the winter, enough to freeze the nuts off a D-9 bulldozer, serving no good purpose—there are no bugs or stink to blow away.

Later, in the spring, clouds of birds arrive—water birds up from other continents to carry on life's continuum in the ever-yellow grass that fights the flat wind. Cranes, geese, ducks, shorebirds and cotton-necked tundra swans; rafts and flights, swarms of broken V's, a frontal system of waterfowl, with the noise of spring like distant shouting. You can see them there now in that same way as 10,000 years ago; and the people too, striking the first meat of spring and burying eggs to ripen mellow.

In the summer, it's up the river to fish camp, and Yup'ik families in white canvas tents along the willow banks make smoker fires and mend nets for the king salmon drifts. Pilot bread and canned butter and strawberry jam taste like you remember, and boiled coffee on a gasoline stove and cut fish drying in the perfume of a red-willow smoke are aromas of something you knew before.

The great, brown, moving water sounds like sifting sand, which it is; and along the bank, fish are running beneath the surface, but you can't see them. The current boils out where it's deep. A kicker motor whines like a mosquito, a constant throb, like a skiff circling empty; and I don't care if you can swim, the river silt will weigh you down and smother your lungs with the brown water you love.

Up the Innoko fork is old Iditarod. Auriferous hills there, wanting to remain silent; creeks asking anonymity lest they fall to the grind of the dredge—that bloated barge abandoning boulders in the wake of its torment. And in this old turn-of-the-century gold camp, there are chalky board buildings too stark even for ghosts, but remembering young girls who came all the way from Crooked Creek on the Kuskokwim, just to dance; and it's like they never left, because the silence there and steep wind down between the buildings say it cannot be so lonely as this; and the mind seeks visions just to keep the soul from dying. Girls dancing in the night.

Jim Fleming was there when I last saw the place, he and his two boys and a baby. He gave me an old goose-neck coffee pot made in 1917, one a grizzly had gripped with his teeth. Jim's wife was in the hospital far away after scalding herself with boiling water. Jim was moving farther back into the mountains. "Too many people around," he said. But there wasn't anyone else, just sounds of creek water running. And echoes of dancing girls.

CHAPTER THIRTEEN

The Bethel Experience

*There was another little lake behind the old hospital,
but you needed to be low on fuel, be alone, and have a
decent wind to fly out of there....*

Mosquitoes love the aroma of aviation gas. They are drawn to the fumes as bees to flowers. Fueling a float plane along the mosquito-infested Yukon River, pouring gas from a five-gallon tin through a chamois-filtered funnel while balanced on a sometimes wet wing, educates me to the maddening insistence of the intoxicated mosquito. It's a two-handed job, fueling that way. Swatting at mosquitoes will result in sloshing the fuel out of the funnel or losing the can over the side. Not as disastrous as swatting a fly with the same hand as the one you're using to shave with while holding a straight razor, but nevertheless, the only thing slicker than a rain-wet metal wing is a metal wing wet with avgas slopped on it.

While flying the Yukon-Kuskokwim river deltas on fisheries patrol with a Cessna 180, I would use as much as seventy-five gallons of fuel a day, most of it from five-gallon cans, the only fuel available in the smaller villages out there. At first, early in the season, there was always someone to help carry the cans from the store down to river's edge, and even hand them up to you one at a time while you fueled the wing tanks. The helper would keep the cans in trade for helping. They could be used for a lot of things: patching a roof, storing goods, hauling water, or carrying extra gas for the small skiffs. Later in the summer, however, as the villages became glutted with my cans, I couldn't find anyone who needed them. So I would do the fueling by myself.

It worked like this: Haul the ten to fifteen cans down to the river, two at a time, from wherever the store is located in the village. Take one can and climb onto the left float, stepping up on the first foot peg and hoisting the can up, carefully setting it on top the engine cowling; step to the next peg with the left foot, extending the right foot across to the strut to balance yourself; pick up the can on the cowling and hoist it across to the wing; finally, climb up to the wing and dump the fuel into the funnel. Then you're ready to climb down to get another can. I think of it now as a young man's job. I thought of it then as just another necessary step to getting back in the air and enjoying the work I loved.

I marveled at the people who would go to work for us and end up not liking the job, or use it as a stepping stone to a more cushy position in the bureaucracy. I never understood it. It seemed to me a perfect way to make a living—out in the woods, being paid to do something others spent their off-time and vacations doing. It didn't pay well at the time, but it didn't matter to me as long as I could provide the essentials for my family. Studies show that pay isn't the most important factor once the employee is making enough to furnish food, shelter, and clothing for himself and his family. After that, it's quality of work environment. Pissanting cans up to the wing and swatting mosquitoes was a part of the quality of work to me. Later, when I was stuck in an office from eight to five and mowing the grass on weekends, I missed the smell of avgas, bug dope, fresh delta winds, the methodical moving tempo of the villagers, and the peaceful freedom of flight. Without those pleasures, I knew the plight of the caged bird.

If you have to stay in Bethel, the largest village on the lower Kuskokwim River, you might long for the hills.

You could be a flatlander even, but still not care for Bethel. If you were raised there and had family around, you might feel differently, but even then you may think it preferable to be somewhere else, even if you had never been somewhere else. It's probably just a state-of-mind, but for those who feel that way, it could be symbolic of the muddy terrain, the muddy river, and the muddy skies.

The surrounding land itself is interesting yet beautiful in its own way, however, but is best described in good black and white photography: tundra, bogs and windy lakes; straight skylines, gray roily river with soft silt bars of stick willows; sheer cutbanks exposing the black melt of permafrost and folds of overhanging muskeg. The winds are cold. It is a land horizoned in the spring and summer with heavy flights of waterfowl and sweltering fogs of gnats and mosquitoes.

Bethel is built on the wrong side of the river—the cutbank side, where it gradually gives itself away to the undermining Kuskokwim. The town has eaten millions of federal and state dollars as governments try to accomplish the impossible: stop the natural erosion process of this powerful, meandering river which wants and needs to flow in that direction. God would have to erase some of the laws of nature in order to stop it himself. Old car bodies, wringer washers, and scrap metal (among other particulars) are dumped along the bank to divert the current—a junkyard in the town's front yard. In addition, as if the junk yard appearance isn't enough, when the river floods each year, it washes the town dump, which is situated up-river, down through the community.

❦

Bethel was *wet* when I was there (Alaska jargon, meaning you could buy, sell, and keep booze). The surrounding villages, the smaller villages all over the Yukon and Kuskokwim deltas, were *dry*; therefore, the alcoholics gravitated to Bethel, where they ended up staying since they couldn't afford to leave, nor did their home villages want them back, for that matter. So Bethel had more than its fair share of drunks hanging around, which didn't help its image or the scenery either.

While in Bethel, we officers stayed in a fish net shed belonging to the Commercial Fisheries Division. It was on the edge of town and along the caving river bluff. The amount of sand in there was incredible. But there was an old couch that folded out into a bed, and you could get water delivered, and the honey wagon picked up the sewage. In addition, we could pilfer groceries from the Commercial Fisheries Division's supplies in the shed next door, which wasn't locked: Pilot bread, canned butter, strawberry preserves, Dinty Moore stew, and rice, among other things. Comm Fish was the biggest division in the Fish and Game Department and therefore had lots of money, so they could afford to stake us. I mean, it seemed we were at least entitled to some of the same considerations as the summer hires they had out at the counting towers. In fact, this net shed we stayed in was on loan from Comm Fish. They let us use it just to keep us at their beck and call, I think, to keep us from leaving for somewhere more to our liking—the Catholic Mission at St. Mary's, for example.

But in all fairness to them, they had a point. On the Kuskokwim at Bethel, there were more commercial and subsistence fishermen to contend with and more openings and closures during the fishing seasons. It's where the court system sat, and also the rest of the major government agencies; so, as it turned out, I was stuck there much of the time.

Since I was flying on floats, I had to tie up either along the river (where the airplanes were subject to sabotage or vandalism) or at one of two nearby lakes: "H" Marker Lake out by the airport or another little lake behind the old hospital (though you needed to be low on fuel, be alone, and have a decent wind to fly out of there). If you had a passenger or a load to pick up, you would have to do it on the river. The hospital lake was the closer one to the old net shed, so we used it more often because we usually had to walk. We fueled down on the river in narrow Brown's Slough over by Lousetown—Lousetown being on the other side of the slough from the rest of town, sniffed at by the locals as though it represented the wrong side of the tracks, although I defy anyone to tell the difference, and if God ever sent me to Bethel after I died, I'd probably pick Lousetown for my accommodations if He gave me a choice.

You could taxi into Brown's Slough from off the river, thread your way through three or four Cessna 180s docked there at Jimmix Samuelson's Flying Service, tie up to the dock and get some fuel. All Jimmix's airplanes had wing-tip and tail damage from constantly banging into each other, and I was certain ours would look that way too, in time. I didn't have too many flight hours on floats then, so I suppose I thought it was normal to have to slip around in places such as that (and it seemed tame compared to the trees coming down the Koyukuk River at Bettles). It was a trial—I think even now—a trial to keep from causing too much damage to my airplane or theirs, especially when alone and having to cut the engine, climb out onto the wing, run out to the end to push off one of the other planes you were headed for due to the wind or the river current having changed or because of the tide flow, or because you miscalculated as you taxied into the slough. Then, there was also the breakwater wall opposite the float dock which was higher than the wings at low tide. I still have bad dreams about squeezing through there.

Eventually we moved the float plan operation to Hangar Lake, which was out past the dump on the road that led from Lousetown. It was a few miles out there, and sometimes we had to walk, especially when the road was washed out, but the plane was safer. A year or two later, we set up a 500 gallon tank for our fuel there. That was when we had a vehicle to use, a couple of officers assigned there for part of the season, and a decent place for them to stay.

※

It was at Hangar Lake that I had my first episode with—how shall I say it?—with my digestive tract. Without going into a great deal of physiological and personal medical deficiencies, suffice it to say it was something the doctors couldn't do anything about at the time. If I ate anything, it was obligatory that I not fly within an hour of that time; after that, there was usually no problem. It took some grave instances though before that bit of information finally sunk in. It took a couple of really bad episodes, in fact, before I became a believer. Most people need to learn only once that a potent laxative is nothing to fool around with. The laxative in this case was just food. Not always though. It wasn't a predictable occurrence by any means, but you could almost depend on it if you were going to be in a location that precluded finding somewhere to relieve yourself—like a 1,000 feet up in the sky in a small airplane.

The first time the inevitable happened, I was flying the Lower Kuskokwim River commercial fishing season in our Cessna 180 on floats. I had eaten lunch in the air somewhere on the lower river, had worked my way up toward Bethel, and was about five minutes away from there when nature called—was calling. The big river was full of small skiffs—fishermen fishing their drift nets and going to and from their set nets—so I knew I couldn't land there, tie up along the bank somewhere, and run into the willows in time. It was that bad. The only other alternative was to head directly for Hangar Lake. There wouldn't be the necessity of having to hunt for cover—there wasn't any cover at Hangar Lake—but there likely might be more privacy. To grasp an idea of the difference between the river and the lake at that particular time of year, just imagine your choice of squatting alongside an interstate freeway at rush hour, versus your own back yard in town at, say, three in the afternoon. Neither an outstanding choice, but you could hope that none of the neighbors would be at home or looking out their windows.

I wasted no time at Hangar Lake with anything resembling a standard landing approach. I beelined in the shortest route there, taking a quick look at the wind direction. (The wind direction on a lake is not difficult to determine; you look for the smooth water. Whichever bank the smooth water is located next to, you land toward that bank.) I made an unsophisticated, fast landing; kept the 180 on a high step all the way to my tie-down; dropped off the step at the last moment; drove the airplane up snug on the sand so I wouldn't have to take valuable time to tie it; grabbed a roll of paper out of the back seat as I stumbled out the door; jumped off the floats and ran (you wouldn't call it wading) through the shallow water and on up into the blueberry bushes next to the road—a singleness of purpose, if you will.

It was my good fortune to find the entire lake devoid of people, even though there were several other planes tied to the same shoreline. So far, so good; though I don't know how it could have turned out any different if there had been a football game going on—it was time.

You must know how it is when it's time, when you've waited to where you simply can't stand it any longer, and you're saying your prayers, and trying to tell yourself that it's alright, there really isn't any hurry, and you try very hard to truly believe the lie you're telling yourself isn't a lie. But the body knows otherwise, and the body has been doing its best, but is satisfied that you've finally made it to your destination and by then there's nothing that can stop the call.

Nothing except a stuck zipper.

The uniform coveralls I was wearing had always zippered perfectly, but as I reached my place of deposit (my body and my mind both tremendously relieved, though still trying to hold on just one more second), the zipper hung about an inch into the unzip and wouldn't budge. There was no room for even the thought of *This can't be happening!* or *I wonder what's wrong with this zipper?* My mind was at its finest adrenaline tuning—this was more serious than a gun call to a family disturbance—the reaction was automatic, but it wasn't my weapon I reached for, it was my Buck knife on my trousers belt just inside the right pocket opening of the coveralls. I whipped the knife out, pried open the long blade, and slashed the coveralls open from the neck all the way to the knee on the right leg. How I kept from eviscerating myself, I have no idea. But the outcome was total relief.

What I hadn't considered—not that it mattered a whit—was that my coveralls, thrown back behind as I assumed the position that we all have to take every day, were in such a way as to receive the brunt of the results.

With the coveralls sliced from neck to knee, there was no problem carefully extricating myself; however, I have to admit publicly now, after all this time, that I didn't retrieve the remnants of the coveralls. I couldn't just leave them there with identifying shoulder patches shining out at anybody who walked by, so I did the next best thing—I gingerly took my life-saving Buck knife and cut off the sleeves (the evidence as it were) and shoved the rest of the coveralls under a blueberry bush in hopes they would be considered biodegradable.

You would think there would be something to learn from that.

The next and the last episode, at least of any significance, was some months later in the dead of winter. I was flying a Super Cub that time, and had eaten lunch in Aniak just thirty minutes previous to the incident, when I had a familiar sensation. It was too late to return to Aniak. I was up near the headwaters of the Aniak River in the Kilbuck Hills. There were some nice frozen lakes up there I could land on, but the wind was on its worst behavior across the glacier-blue surfaces. Once again, there wasn't any choice. I dropped down and landed on a barren, moon-scaped lake, jumped out and found that the wind was blowing so hard I had to hang onto a wing strut to stay upright. This was a new take on freezing your tail off. But this time I had no coveralls to contend with. They were degrading under the wind-swept snow somewhere near the town of Bethel.

CHAPTER FOURTEEN

Pilot's Code of the North

I come in low over the two frosted figures, maybe a hundred feet, banking as I pull over them. Their upturned faces are purple against the snow underfoot.

There's an unwritten Code of the North for Alaskan flyers: drop whatever you are doing and go search if an aircraft is missing or overdue. This is especially relevant in winter. If it's forty below zero with only four hours of daylight, time is a hard factor. It doesn't matter who is missing, friend or not—an Alaska pilot simply goes.

Unfortunately, there are exceptions....

On November 1, 1971, a single-engine Maule airplane with two Aniak men on board encountered a heavy snow squall about dark along the Kuskokwim River. With visibility down to almost zero forward, the pilot swung the aircraft around and tried to find the snow-covered river bar he saw a ways back. He located the bar, but disoriented by the blinding snow, landed across the snow-covered island rather than down the length of it, getting dunked bottom-side-up in the slush-choked river water.

Both men on board, thinking they would have to swim, remove their boots and scramble out of the sinking Maule onto the fabric covered wings as it rotates like a soggy birch leaf down the big river laden with the mushy circles of freeze-up ice. They haven't had time to get the emergency gear

– 91 –

out with them, and only think frantically of getting off a sinking death trap that only minutes before was a warm haven of soft glowing lights and droning, lulling engine. As one wing swings around toward the bank of the island, they both jump off into waist-deep water and struggle up onto the snow-covered, barren island in their wet, stocking feet. They don't have a single match or cigarette lighter between them. It is twenty-five degrees with a wind out of the south at fifteen mph, bringing the chill down to thirteen degrees. It will get much colder that night.

I get a call sometime after midnight from the Federal Aviation Administration flight service office telling me the aircraft is overdue on a round-robin flight out of Aniak, a village 150 miles downriver from McGrath where I live at the time. It's early winter, starting to freeze hard at night, and we're experiencing the first heavy snowfall of the season—not a good time to be out. The report is that the overdue air-taxi pilot had been chartered to make a booze run upriver from Aniak, a dry village. The flight would be eighty miles to Red Devil where a liquor store was located, the only one along a 300 mile stretch of the Kuskokwim River from McGrath to Bethel. A check at Red Devil finds that the two men had made it there and left on the return leg back to Aniak. That's the last anyone has seen of them. The temperature is sixteen degrees with ten inches or so of fresh snow on the ground when I take off at daylight to see if I can find them.

It's an hour and a half straight across the hills to Crooked Creek or the Red Devil Mine, closer to two hours if the winding river has to be followed due to bad weather. The snow clouds are still hugging some of the hills as I fly somewhat straight across and reach the Kuskokwim River just upriver from Red Devil. There I start my search. The Super Cub is ideal for searching the ground, having plenty of visibility from either side and a slow flying-speed; however, this is one of those overcast days, making things on the fresh snow shadowless, gray, and undefinable.

Downstream, near Crooked Creek, I make contact on the emergency frequency with an Air Force Rescue C130 Hercules out of Elmendorf Air Force Base. They say they are in the area at 200 feet, and want to know my position. *Two hundred feet?* I wonder what the hell they are doing down at 200 feet in that big four-engine propped monster—*four Super Cub-eating props*, I think, since I'm also at 200 feet. I quickly pull up to about the 600 foot level. In a few minutes they sail by underneath, following the meanderings of the river, looking as out of place as a giant sperm whale in a trickle of snow melt. I talk to them.

There are no other local aircraft besides mine flying the search that morning, they tell me, which seems a little strange out here in the bush—or anywhere, for that matter, when a plane is missing.

After rounding a long bend in the river near the abandoned fish camps at Napaimiut, not far down the river from our passing, they call that they've spotted something; then I see it myself—objects moving on a snow-covered bar up ahead, two dark forms in a foot of cotton under a gray sky. They are waving in frantic gestures as though they're afraid they haven't been seen, though the Herc has turned to come back (finally climbing up out of Super Cub territory) and I am pointing my nose toward the island the two men stand on, less than a mile away. I come in low over the two frosted figures, maybe a hundred feet, banking as I pull over them. Their upturned faces are purple against the snow underfoot. I can see their eyes, and looks of strangulation are there, as though they are looking up at me from beneath water.

It's early in the season and I haven't switched to skis. The airplane is still on large tundra tires; however, I know that the ten or twelve inches of fresh, dry snow is not dangerous if I maintain power and drag it in. Any heavier or wetter snowfall or crusted conditions would eliminate doing this safely. As a precaution, I ask the pilot of the Herc to find out if there are any ski-equipped aircraft available in Aniak, the closest village with an airport downriver. Flight Service in Aniak radios that several planes are on skis, but none are available. So much for the Code of the North.

I land and find both men in their stocking feet and suffering severely. They have spent the night on the windswept, barren, gravel bar huddled together in the snow under the only driftwood tree stump on the island. No shoes, no fire. Feet and hands are frostbitten. It's enough to make a guy swear off the booze.

The C130 is equipped with a doctor and medical supplies, and the pilot agrees to land in Aniak to take these guys to Anchorage. I pick up the two men, having to make two trips because of the snow, and fly them the forty miles or so downriver to the Aniak airstrip, where all the airplanes in town still sit idle. One of the men will have to wait almost an hour for his turn, but the Herc has dropped a survival bundle, and he can at least crawl into a sleeping bag and maybe get something in his stomach.

There are several aircraft owners and another air-taxi operator in Aniak, yet no one has come out to search for these men or help transport them when they've been found. This aberrant behavior is contrary to anything I ever saw or heard of in the bush. Later, it is said that the pilot is a bootlegger and the passenger is the town drunk, and neither of them are liked in the community; the latter being obvious.

I've learned something in all this: I've learned that it will not do for me to be stranded within a hundred miles of the village of Aniak—it's always possible that wildlife officers are no better-liked than bootleggers.

CHAPTER FIFTEEN

Giving Up the Search

*I searched the little headers and canyons that the
missing pilot might possibly mistake for Rainy Pass,
and found nothing.*

The more eyes you have on a search, the better. Observers are nice to have. Still, unless they know what they're looking for, their usefulness is limited. If you are a hunter or an experienced pilot/observer, you know what I mean. A hunter knows he is hunting for moose, say, but until he actually sees a moose in the wild for the first time at a distance, or from high in the air, he only thinks he knows what he's looking for. An experienced hunter will catch the flick of an ear while spotting for game or catch a coloration favorable to what he knows a bull moose looks like, whereas a novice will likely miss it entirely or not know what it is he saw. The experienced search observer will likewise catch some movement on the ground or see the scattered wreckage of an aircraft under snow-covered trees because he has seen those things before, or has been trained to look for them, and can readily pick them out. However, there are exceptions to all that.

I've flown right over stuff that I should have seen—camps and airplanes on the ground in plain sight—and found out about them later. Those are the ones I know of; there have to be others. You can have lots of airplanes and observers, yet still miss what you came to find. And, of course, you have to be looking in the right places.

In 1972 while I am assigned to McGrath, a fifty-year-old pilot from southern California, someone who had never been to Alaska before, turned up missing. He was ferrying a Cessna 172 for a missionary group, as I recall, from California to Kalakaket Creek near Galena, a village on the Yukon River. After several days of flying, he made it in good shape to Soldotna on the Kenai Peninsula. There he refueled and headed out along a route to Galena via Rainy Pass through the Alaska Range. He was dressed in light clothing as if he were going to the laundromat on the outskirts of San Diego maybe. His emergency gear and food consisted of a bedroll and a couple of candy bars. He had no emergency locator transmitter.

The last the FAA knew of him was a weather briefing he was given for his planned route, a trip of over 350 miles wending through the roadless wilderness. It was early May, and there were still winter conditions in the high country through which he was headed. The weather was marginal: low ceilings, low visibility and snow. He filed no flight plan, though he had left information of his long-range intentions with his friends back in California. But he never showed up at his destination at Kalakaket Creek.

We flew for twelve days: the Civil Air Patrol, an Elmendorf Air Force Search and Rescue C-130, myself with a Super Cub, and maybe ten or fifteen other airplanes from villages and outposts along his route; the number of search planes dwindling as time went on. Some of us were concentrating in the Alaska Range, which seemed the most likely country for him to have gotten into trouble. But, after ten or twelve days we had to give it up. It was unlikely he could have survived the freezing temperatures, if nothing else.

There are about five miles of Cook Inlet saltwater that you have to fly across if you're heading for Galena from the Kenai Peninsula, and there was the possibility he might have gone down right there in the drink before he had hardly gotten started. That sort of thing has happened before. Usually there's time to shout for help over the radio, and it's likely someone will hear you, no matter the frequency you happen to be tuned in to, as there is plenty of air traffic in the area. There had been nothing like that in this situation—nothing anyone noticed.

And so we gave it up. We had combed the country relentlessly, every nook and cranny, as far as I could tell. I had zeroed in on the general area of Rainy Pass, because it was the most confusing part of the country he had to navigate, in my estimation. Those of us who know the place know that in poor visibility—the kind he had on the day of his disappearance, snow and low overcast—it would be unlikely he could find the pass, even if he were closely following a sectional chart. I've been fooled more than once approaching that area from the Cook Inlet side. There are a couple of canyon entrances that look the same, and it would be easy to take the wrong one. I wouldn't want to try it if the visibility was poor; the canyon leading up to the pass climbs too fast, and there isn't room in there to turn around at low altitude. Then I would instead go through Ptarmigan Valley, a lower pass, which might take twenty or thirty minutes longer. Ptarmigan is often open when Rainy is socked in. We knew that both of those routes had been marginal at best for flying the day of the disappearance.

With all this in mind, I searched the little headers and canyons that the missing pilot might possibly mistake for Rainy Pass, and found nothing. The search weather was good for the most part.

The day after the search was officially closed, the missing man's family chartered a helicopter in Anchorage to continue the search on their own (a futile sort of thing, it seemed, but something they felt they needed to do). I don't recall who all was on board the chopper, but it was freely admitted later that they didn't know anything about the country or about searching. The pilot was a good one, I suppose, but he was also new to Alaska.

On the day they left Anchorage, they flew directly up into the Alaska Range toward Rainy Pass, a likely place to start, and on up the wide, flat valley that approaches the pass area. Where the valley bends to the left, making a dog-leg, they followed the natural contour of the terrain which leads toward Ptarmigan Pass; but instead of continuing along the Happy River valley in the direction of Ptarmigan, they stayed low and followed a small creek, bending on around until they were pointed back toward a blind mountain in the general direction from which they had come—a giant U-turn. The creek was steeply sloped up to a blind col filled with perpetual snow and ringed by the peaks of a large mountain. A dead end.

In that cereal bowl of gray rock and blue snow, they found the Cessna 172. Inside the airplane they found alive a somewhat weakened Californian, happy to see them. He was taken to the hospital, admitted for observation, and released the next day. He had survived on a couple of candy bars, and conserved heat by staying wrapped in his mummy bag most of the time.

It never occurred to us old hands to look up that little creek, or we would have surely done it. It was pointed in the opposite direction, was very steep and short, but it would have been easy enough to search on a good day from up high with an airplane. It also lay on a direct high altitude air route from Anchorage to Galena via McGrath where anyone could conceivably look down and maybe see him, although it's sometimes difficult to see those things directly below you. He said he saw airplanes up high every day and could hear other planes in the distance frequently, and though he became demoralized, he vowed to stay with the airplane, as he had heard it was the best way to be found. He said he prayed to God.

CHAPTER SIXTEEN

The Hunters

People waste. People in the bush, people from the city; one caribou or fifteen, one bison or millions, one passenger pigeon or all of them. All.

From my airplane I see a scattering of dead caribou—caribou shot and left to lie, fifteen of them. It is in the Western Arctic semi-treeless Baird Mountains, along the upper Squirrel River, a tributary of the lower Kobuk River. The Piper Super Cub leaves a frost contrailing behind in the twenty-five below zero air; I see it shadowed against the bright snow. I can still sense the aroma from those days of cold flight: the smell of home-tanned chopper mitts heated by the defroster on top of the instrument panel, the odor of ignited 80/87 octane fuel and pungent nondetergent engine oil. The air is smooth; the sun etches the definition of tracks in the snow. Perfect for tracking four-legged animals and two-legged poachers.

Two of the caribou have been salvaged; some of the others have been dragged to a central location but not eviscerated. The gases have bloated them; the birds, the ravens and Canada jays, have worked on them. The snowmachine tracks lead to the village of Selawik, out on the flats, sixty-plus miles away.

One man there is the successful hunter; he is not hard to find. The village has been needy of meat, so everyone knows who has been successful; however, it's doubtful they know just how successful this man has been. He hasn't shared any of the meat he brought back from his hunt. He is sleeping off a drunk after celebrating his accomplishment, when I find him. You might think he would have led the other villagers to the kill site, but that didn't happen. He had located the herd of caribou while scouring the countryside on his snowmachine. He killed and killed with his high-powered rifle; he killed until his ammunition ran out. He field-dressed and loaded two caribou on his sled, leaving the rest, and returned to the village. He never went back. Maybe the caribou would be closer than sixty miles next time, or maybe not. This event was near the beginning of a rapid population decline in the Western Arctic caribou herds. Wolves, over-hunting, starvation, disease, and mismanagement would take their toll on the animals. It would be years before there was a plentiful supply again.

∾

Not more than twenty miles up the Holitna River from its junction with the Kuskokwim River at the village of Sleetmute, I spot the black form of a moose contrasting against the gray-white of the river ice, seemingly in repose. But this moose is different from the other moose I have been seeing on my all-day flying patrol out of McGrath this January day. This moose on the snow is dead.

Descending 300 or 400 feet off the river, I can see that it is a young bull, apparently left untouched. As I circle to land, I spot another carcass a couple of hundred yards downstream. This one has the hindquarters removed. Airplane ski tracks are visible intermittently in a few soft snow drifts along the hard ice of the river surface. I land off to one side to keep from disturbing what sign there is.

Once on the ground, I need to make quick work of my inspection. The temperature is about forty below zero here on the river, and though dressed for the cold, I know that my feet will begin to freeze after thirty minutes or so in the winter shoepacs I am wearing. Twenty-five below is about their limit. Of course, if worse comes to worst, I can dig my trail mukluks out of the emergency gear in the back of the airplane. I cover the engine with the cowl cover to retain some of its heat, a habit this time of year even when I only plan a short stop. It would not do to have a frozen-up engine out here in the middle of nowhere.

The sign on the snow reads like a book. A ski/wheel Cessna 180 or 185, according to the shape of the skis tracks and the distance between them, had dropped off two people, then took off and herded the two moose from downriver around the bend to the two hunters waiting in ambush in the willows off to the side. Six total shots from a 30.06 and a .270 had dropped both moose. The airplane then returned, the pilot helping the other two hunters remove the hindquarters of one bull and load them into the plane. They did not touch the second animal.

In addition to the boot prints of all three individuals, the brass cartridge cases, and the ski tracks, I find two additional items of evidence: some Kleenex with yellow decoration along the borders and a custom-made, sheath-style hunting knife left at the butchered carcass.

The kills are several days old; the birds have been picking at the carcasses and defecating on them. The poachers will likely not be coming back for the rest of the meat. There are several violations here: taking moose out of season, wasting game meat, harassing and herding game with an aircraft.

There are many possible places to start looking for these characters. Anchorage has the biggest resident number of aircraft in the state. It lies about 300 miles from where I stand. A good possibility, which might explain why the poachers hadn't returned for the rest of the meat; however, it's a long way to go to poach moose in the first place, and there is plenty of game much closer to town.

Bethel, with a fair number of ski-equipped airplanes, lies about 150 miles the other direction. There are fewer moose around Bethel, but still plenty of them closer than the Holitna country. No, these boys are going to be from around the immediate area here somewhere—somewhere, say within fifty miles, which includes some seven or eight villages.

Most of the airplanes privately owned in the bush at that time are smaller than the Cessna 180 or 185, and most people do not own the more expensive ski/wheel combination, a combination which allows the pilot to land on either snow or a dry, hard surface. In fact, about the only ones who own this sort of plane are air taxi operators. I know most of these operators, and I doubt that any of them would be involved in such shenanigans. But it's still the best hunch.

I fly downriver to Red Devil, a tiny settlement below Sleetmute, where the nearest air taxi operator with a plane that size lives. He says he doesn't know anything about the illegal moose, but gives me consent to search his Cessna 180 on ski/wheels. A Kleenex box with yellow trimmed paper is there; the knife sheath matching the knife left at the scene is there; bits of blood, meat, and moose hair are there. He is cooperative, and says his son has had exclusive use of the plane for the last week or so. The father and I talk to the nineteen-year-old son, who admits to the crime and implicates two others, a school teacher and a local contractor, both from Sleetmute. All three are wage earners and of varied ethnic background. They give no reason for wasting the meat left on the river, but pay hefty fines in the McGrath court for doing so.

☙

I need to remind myself, now and then—whenever I get the urge to blame any particular segment of the population for wasting game animals—that the Western European brought over firearms to this country, and with them the true beginnings of large-scale waste. As far back as 1881, naturalist John Muir, while aboard the U.S. Revenue steamer *Thomas Corwin* in the Chukchi Sea off the west coast of Alaska, wrote of his fear that the native caribou had been "well-nigh exterminated within the last few years" by repeating rifles traded by whalers to the villagers for ivory, whalebone, and furs. The native Alaskan could kill only so many caribou with a spear or snare. The repeating rifle gave him a new ability. The snowmachine gave us all a new ability, as did the airplane and the motorboat. It allowed some people to trample on the spirit of the hunting privilege.

People waste. People in the bush, people from the city; one caribou or fifteen, one bison or millions, one passenger pigeon or all of them. All.

☙

From my patrol aircraft, I see the four quarters of a moose hanging under a spruce scaffold near the bank of a small river—Highpower Creek, a tributary of the Slow Fork of the Kuskokwim River. There is a camp there. Smoke from a smudge fire floats over the meat, keeping the flies away. There is a wooden river skiff tied to the bank. The handmade skiff and lack of trash or modern accouterments indicate this is poor man's camp. Poor, but thrifty. And, it is a permanent camp, by the looks of the well-trodden ground, the size of the fire pit, and the gray of the cache poles and fish-drying racks. It is not moose season (at least by the laws made by urban dwellers); it is too early in the fall. I land on some open turf not far from the camp.

A young Athabascan and two small children come to meet me. We go to the camp for coffee. His wife is there, and a baby. The camp is clean and the early sun steams the damp river bank. There is a view from here, out across the boggy flats beyond the clearwater river, where you can see the rounded tops of the Telida Hills towards Lake Minchumina—hills turning gold and orange from the early fall birch. He does not mention the moose hanging nearby. He can see very well who I am.

We visit; I want to know what he does. He lives here year-round with his family. He does not wish to live at Nicholai, his village many miles downriver; there is too much violence there, he says. There is too much drinking in the village and too much laziness, he says. He has lived here at this camp for three years. He traps for fur in the winter, makes his own snowshoes out of willow and sinew, traps sheefish in the summer for his winter dog feed, teaches his oldest son the things his grandfather taught him. I know he feels a pride in his abilities, and a sense of worth.

We talk about the moose. His grandfather has taught him this is the time to kill the moose for the best meat, before the rut. He doesn't care about the antlers; they don't make good soup. He says he's fortunate to have found the moose so early before the snows, but he knows the season isn't open yet, and has heard there are game wardens who enforce such rules.

I tell him before I go to not leave his moose near the river bank for everyone who flies by to see. I tell him that someone may see it and turn him in, and that it will mean the loss of the meat and a month or more in jail away from his family. I tell him that if I come by here again and see a moose, I will take him to jail. I do not smile, because it is a serious thing for me. This is the first time in my long career as a wildlife officer that I will overlook what in most places is a serious game violation. He does not smile either. He understands what I am saying, the totality of it. His son smiles up at me. He's too young to know what we are saying, yet he needs reassurance that his father and this lawman are not too engrossed in serious talk to forget about the pleasantries of life, and that it is a good day.

I fly back by in a week or so. The moose is not in sight. I waggle my wings and go on.

CHAPTER SEVENTEEN

Wheels on Water

We were well out over the center of the river when we began sinking back toward the surface.

An airplane is like any other machine manually controlled—if you use it a lot, it may seem to become a part of you. A forklift operator, a truck driver, or a typist will become so adept at operating their particular machine that it serves as an extension of themselves, like an arm or a leg.

An old government trapper friend of mine who was an artist of the quick-draw could hit anything he pointed his Colt single-action revolver at, and from the hip. It was a simple thing, he said. He practiced and used the weapon so much that it had become a part of his hand. He would say, "Point your finger at that doorknob while you're relaxed...do it from the hip or anywhere else from where your hand is resting; you'll see that the finger, if you sort of bend down to where you can sight down it, will be pointing directly at the doorknob. That's because the hand and the eye are coordinated perfectly." His long-barreled, single-action .45 had become his pointing finger.

Anyway, for someone who constantly manipulates a machine or tool, it may not only be the hand/eye coordination, but a total body coordination with that item. A good forklift operator is an artist with his machine—a ballet dancer in blue collar. It's the same for a good pilot. But a critical difference with an airplane is it likely won't be as forgiving if you make a mistake. You may not be able to go back and do it over.

Flight is sensational; yet, it isn't normal to understand the dynamics from a sensation level. Only in your dreams does flying seem simple and free—it's there that you're not so far removed from the birds in spirit, maybe. We value the sensation of flying and understand it in our subconsciousness; but in our awakened state, it's an impossible understanding. The airship is a tool to gain the wings of what we have envisioned. Learning to fly is unlearning some natural reactions. It is natural to want to pull up if the aircraft is stalling and falling. The opposite is true. In order to build flying speed and gain life-sustaining lift for you and the aircraft, you push forward on the controls. With enough practice it becomes a common reflex, and it needs to be a reflex, because if you're low enough to the ground, there won't be time to think about the right way to react. Pilots rightfully fear stalling near the ground—it isn't the air above you that counts. There may not be room beneath you to recover.

Becoming comfortable with flying is a wonderful feeling; that's when you believe you've mastered those learned reactions and feel they are now natural to you. But there's still a variable that you need to consider: it's not like walking or swimming or mastering the piano or typewriter even, where you know and sense the body's limitations and coordinations. The variable is the airplane itself—you are limited to that particular airplane's limitations in that given atmosphere (an atmosphere that is constantly changing). A tight, steep, slow turn that feels perfectly natural and comfortable in a certain airplane today, may kill you tomorrow. It's why even some of the more experienced pilots die in stalls near the ground.

While based out of McGrath, I had been patrolling the hunting seasons by air in the Kuskokwim and Stony River watersheds along the western slopes of the Alaska Range. I was flying constantly, eight or nine hours a day, and my Piper Super Cub had become a part of me, that extended arm or leg. The airplane would simply perform to whatever degree I wanted it to. That was my frame of mind, anyway, and what I had fooled myself into believing, no doubt.

I had placed two wildlife officers on a week-long surveillance stakeout for illegal hunting activities on Little Underhill Creek, a small river actually, which lies between the Stony and Swift rivers, and drains some rough and little-touched country on the west side of the Alaska Range. The officers were there to monitor the activities of a couple of unscrupulous guides who were known to frequent the area, and who weren't above taking an illegal moose, bear, or caribou. I had radio contact with the officers each night to see if they had seen anything, and by the end of the week, I decided I could better use their talents over on the other side of Sled Pass in the Hartman River country, so I let them know I'd be picking them up in the morning.

When I got to Little Underhill, I found they had relocated a few miles downstream to a place that afforded a better observation point from which to see up and down the valley. That was fine with me; a gravel bar there afforded a landing area. However, the length of the bar didn't look ideal for takeoff due to a rock bluff sticking up a couple of hundred feet into the air at the downhill end where the river made a sharp bend to the left.

It wasn't an insurmountable problem, however, as there appeared to be enough room to take off across the width of the gravel bar. And across the river was a longer bar which would be better for removing each man and all his gear. I asked one of them, Leon Steele, to tote the gear across via a wide, shallow, upstream ford, and I would take the other officer, Paul Seibel, for a quick flight up the canyon to check out a possible illegal moose kill. A plane had gone up there the day before, some shots had been heard by the officers, and later the plane was seen leaving with a moose rack tied to the strut. We wanted to see if they had taken all the meat, or were just trophy killers. It was legal at that time to shoot moose and caribou on the same day a hunter was flying, but the meat had to be salvaged.

With Paul in the back seat, I figured that with half tanks of fuel and no extra gear I could take off across the bar, out over, and straight down the river. After all, up to then the airplane had simply been doing whatever I wanted it to do.

After pulling the tail back into the bushes to give myself plenty of room, and after applying full power before releasing the brakes, I began the takeoff run, holding the plane on the ground right up to the edge of the water to gain all the flying speed possible. Then, I popped it off with flaps and was airborne—but only for a few seconds. We were well out over the center of the river when we began sinking back toward the surface ("sinking" is a word that could describe either the feeling in my stomach, the motion of the aircraft, or what was going to happen to us when we reached the water).

Although the river was not extremely deep, probably three to four feet in that spot, it was fast, and its direction carried it toward swift and rocky rapids a few hundred yards downstream. There could not be much to salvage from a brand new stick and rag airplane suffering the fate this river had to offer. However, those were not my thoughts at the moment. I had all my fleeting, wide-eyed thoughts concentrated on keeping the engine at full power, and hugging the control stick all the way back into my stomach.

The large balloon tundra tires rolled along the surface, gathering up more and more water, before we began settling to the bottom. The propeller dug into the river as the nose went down and the tail came up. Leon, who was back on the takeoff bar, said later there was so much water blown into the air he lost sight of the plane for an instant, and knew that the next thing he would see was an upside-down Super Cub floating down the river.

The left gear settled to the bottom first, and I could feel the tire bumping along the rocks and gravel. The engine was still at full throttle and I could see nothing but water spraying up, over, around, and into the cockpit. Now came the part that defies explanation by anyone I know made of flesh, blood, and bones. The airplane was back out of the water and flying.

The aircraft had come back up out of a nose-down, water-bogged attitude in three to four feet of water, and it was flying, ever so slowly, and hanging by the prop, right on down the river. I remember turning it slowly toward the left, and we bounced to a stop on the gravel bar across and to the side of the river, the engine still running. I looked back at Paul in the back seat and asked, "Are you okay?"

"Yes," he said, but he looked pale as a stiff, water dripping from his nose and chin—river water inside the cockpit!

A Super Cub needs a little over forty miles an hour of air speed to fly. Ours did not have the speed necessary to hold it in the air in the first place; that's why it settled back to the surface. Although the river was swift, it was certainly not rolling faster than forty miles an hour, and therefore could only have served as additional drag, slowing the aircraft even more, and if anything, slowing it very quickly to the velocity of the river. The wind did not appear to be a factor as there were no gusts to the light breeze. The Cub simply came back up out of the water and flew, defying all human knowledge and the scientific laws of flight dynamics.

I shut down the engine and we got out to inspect the damage. Nothing. Leon was back there on the other side of the river jumping up and down, shouting and waving. A normally quiet individual, he was hopping up and down on the gravel bar, making noise. He couldn't believe we were alright.

Paul and I hand-tracked the propeller through; no damage anywhere—nothing. We cleared a few stumps out of the way and took off. Only nerves had been shattered (and some vague notions about the airplane being a natural extension of myself).

CHAPTER EIGHTEEN

Little Joe's Worst Day

The far end of the lake is coming up fast—he can see the old man and his dog off to one side, frozen as though in a photograph.

From Sled Pass, at the head of the Stony River, it's a straight shot almost all the way to where the river escapes the Alaska Range and opens out into the lower hills, working its way toward its confluence with the Kuskokwim River another hundred miles downstream. There's a smallish lake on the upper end of the Stony we call Brantley Lake. For good reason.

Little Joe Brantley was a friend to everybody, even to the worst of the poachers and bandit guides (which didn't preclude him from arresting any of them, and they knew it). Joe was a state wildlife trooper based out of Anchorage during most of his career, though he wasn't a stranger to the bush—spent every minute out there he could, was an experienced pilot, and was savvy about the ways of the people and the wildlife. Joe was a guy who didn't look the part of the Alaskan outdoorsman/game warden, at least not what most people think of as the type. It wasn't necessarily because Joe was short in stature and round as a keg of beer, nor was it that Joe always wore a big grin and had that look—how can I describe it—that hayseed look of an Oklahoma country boy (which he was), with sunshine-burnt hide, and a Heinz 57 pedigree of about everything mid-western American mixed up in him. It was like Joe had the farm belt wrapped up inside enough to where it boiled over in a roughness of features, and you expected at any time to have to brush straw out of his hair—hair that looked like his mother tried to slick it back before he went to church, but hair that had finally had its own way eventually during the Sunday morning services, struggling and springing back to the position in which it was most comfortable—a tousled lock of it hanging in his face, like Will Rogers or Charlie Russell, maybe.

And Joe, even though he spent his fair share of time in the woods, never seemed to be dressed for the part. He wore the uniform more or less in the appropriate manner alright, but usually had on low-cut, street shoes wherever he went, winter or summer, rain or shine, mud or snow, forty below zero or sixty-five above. In the winter, he'd land his patrol airplane equipped with skis on a frozen river along a trapline somewhere 200 miles from town, and gingerly hop out in his wingtips and thin socks, a big grin on his face, to jaw with some crusty trapper as though they were on a dry sidewalk in downtown Fairbanks on the 4th of July. The trapper, of course, would know Joe and be tickled to see him. Though he would notice that Joe was in street shoes and a light jacket, he probably didn't expect to see him any other way. It was said Joe was the only officer alive who was welcome to walk into a state Supreme Court justice's office without knocking, and be just as warmly greeted by an Athabascan or Yup'ik hunter out on the Kuskokwim River somewhere; nor would he be dressed differently or present himself differently in either place.

Joe didn't carry any emergency gear when he flew, which wasn't smart. He would just smile if you asked him about it, or if you made some remark like, "Joe, you crazy? What's gonna happen if the bird conks out on you...How you gonna survive?" It was like he always knew that wasn't the way he would eventually go, and of course it wasn't. He went at the age of 46, lying in a hospital bed with the slow pain of colon cancer eating away inside him, the technicians jabbing him with bone marrow needles, while he hollered at them to leave him the hell alone. He couldn't talk by then, only scream unintelligible things, though I know he was fully lucid, in spite of his mutterings when he was at rest, like there was a chill running through his body that he could not control. And when he was hollering for them not to hurt him again with the damned bone needle, he would be wanting some of us to help him get rid of the insensitive slobs who were doing it—kick some butt and take some names and defend his right to die in peace—but we didn't. And once when he indicated he needed to pee and wanted me to help with the bed pan, I was too embarrassed, I guess, and went running down the hall to get a nurse, or somebody to help. By the time I got back, he had made a mess, and I felt like a damned fool, as if I'd let him down—the only request he ever made of me. But he looked at me as if to say it was alright and that he understood and probably would have done the same thing if the shoe was on the other foot. I couldn't believe his eyes then, but I do now. I loved him like a brother.

But, anyway, where was I? Oh, I was going to tell about Joe's worst couple of days ever as a pilot. He would always start the story out that way, "Did I ever tell you about my worst two days?"

∽

It was back several years before he died. He was taking some time off from the job and had agreed to ferry a new Cessna 180 from Anchorage out across the Alaska Range and down the Kuskokwim River to Bethel for an air taxi friend he knew out there, a fellow by the name of Jimmix. Jimmix would pay him a few bucks, but Joe didn't care so much about that; he'd have done it for nothing, just to fly, just as a favor to the guy, and just to get a chance to visit a few old friends along the way. Which brings to mind that Joe wasn't happy doing things alone. He would do them, but he preferred company.

So it was his good fortune to run into an old trapper friend—a guy he mentioned only by the name of Jack—down on Fourth Avenue, near the courthouse, the day before he was to leave on the ferrying trip. This old fellow had come to town to get his annual supplies and just happened to be heading back to his cabin on the upper Stony River the next day, so Joe said, "I'm headed that way myself...got a one-eighty on floats. Maybe I'll take you. Is there somewhere I can land out there, Jack?"

"Well, sure," said the trapper, "There's a little lake up above my place a few miles. Get me in there, and it'll be just a downhill pack for me." So Joe agreed.

The next day they met at Lake Hood, the seaplane base near Anchorage's International Airport, and loaded up the new Cessna with the trapper, his supplies, and a big black Labrador retriever called Lukey.

When they got over to the Stony, about an hour and a half out of Anchorage, Joe took one look at the little lake that Jack pointed out and figured it was marginal at best. He looked it over, and looked it over, like you do when you're pretty sure the place you're looking at (whether on land or water) just doesn't look right for you. Not *quiiite* big enough or long enough, after you've given it a lot of consideration, flown over and over it, judging and eyeballing it methodically, thinking about the wind direction and speed, the elevation of the landing area, and the density altitude, but none of it giving you a definite answer about whether you should go for it or not (even though the seat of your pants says "no", but your stubborn side has already said "yes").

"Ol' so-and-so went in and out of here three years ago," Jack claims, and naturally, that nudge is all it takes for Joe to make a commitment to land. This is no big deal; it's getting out of that sort of place that you worry about. Maybe you can work it off the water if the wind is right, but what about clearing the obstacles at the end of the lake—the trees and stuff?

◦∽◦

There's a big chocolate-saddled grizzly bear out on the beach as they taxi toward shore. He looks at them, testing the wind with his snout, then ambles off into the trees and brush, sunshine rippling off his silver-tipped guard hairs.

Joe gently eases the floats up on the sand a couple of hundred feet from where the bear was last seen, and he and old Jack off-load Lukey and the gear and groceries. Joe is worrying about the wind some; he'll need a little of it from the right direction to get out of there. But the wind remains calm. He judges his fuel: Fifteen or so gallons used out of the sixty-five he started with; he's still heavy, but it doesn't make sense to drain any out—not yet anyway—he'll save that as his hole card, in case his takeoff doesn't feel right, and he has to abort it.

Joe says goodbye and makes a zigzagging taxi down to the far end of the lake, stirring up the water, creating some bumps that will help break the suction when he is on the step and ready to jockey one float out of the water, and then the other, all in a twisting motion with his left hand, while easing in some flaps with the right to help lift the plane out of the water. He still isn't happy about the wind; there's barely a breeze, so he runs back up the lake part way, once again zigzagging, turns around, and taxies back to the far end in the same manner. He shoves in full throttle then as he is making his final turn taking advantage of the inertia of the taxi, pushes the carb heat off, raises the water rudders after he gets lined out, and goes for it. He has picked an imaginary line across the lake at which he'll abort the takeoff—a bush, I think he said, along the shoreline to the side, serving as a point of reference. He reaches that line, and the decision has to be made immediately: keep going or pull back on the power. He keeps it up. The far end of the lake is coming up fast—he can see the old man and his dog off to one side, frozen as though in a photograph.

Nope!

He shuts her down, but too late. The airplane is not lightening up, and as he pulls off the power and strips the flaps flat, he tries to rock the plane down off the step—needing that breaking action that only the plowing water shoving against the floats can provide when it comes down off the planing step. But no, the beach is coming up quickly and there's too much momentum. The plane finally drops off the step, but it's going to go ashore and there's no way Joe can stop it. So up on the sand it slides, maybe ten or fifteen feet from the water, sitting high and dry.

Now all of a sudden there's that full feeling in the chest, like loneliness, and he knows he's in for the long haul. *How did I get into this predicament anyway? The hell with Alaska and all the crazy trappers, and the air taxi down in Bethel, and the hell with flyin' and all the crap that goes with it, and how come I'm not workin' or sittin' at my desk, and how do I explain all this to ol' Jimmix, the guy who owns this brand new airplane and is trusting me to get it down there to him in one piece?*

It is getting late, maybe eight o'clock already, even though this time of the year it doesn't get totally dark till close to ten-thirty, and lightens up again by three-thirty or so.

The trapper looks the situation over and says he'll make a hike to the cabin with some of his supplies, and pack a come-along back with him. "We'll sink a deadman and jack that rascal around," he says. He has a positive attitude, and it makes Joe feel better and gives him some hope. Old Jack loads up, takes the dog, and heads out. Joe figures he'll stick around in case a smaller plane comes along with some more manpower, because they're going to need it, he knows. Besides, the wingtips and thin socks aren't made for a three or four mile hike off the mountain and back again.

Joe settles down to a long wait, not straying too far from the beached airplane in case he hears another plane and needs to get on the radio. "It looked crazy," he told me later, "There's that one-eighty, bright new paint shining, sittin' high and dry on that little beach, a hundred and fifty miles from the nearest help. I could've got on the HF radio right then, but I figured we could probably get her off the beach ourselves. It was too embarrassing to start broadcasting my predicament all over the countryside."

It starts to get dark, and the old man isn't back. Quite a lot of the groceries are still there, and Joe is thinking now about the grizzly coming around, so he loads the fresh stuff back into the airplane, and after a while climbs in himself. The old man won't be there now till after daylight.

"It gets blacker'n the inside of an Angus cow," Joe says. "I'm just sittin' there dozing on and off, and I'm sorta glad I've got the plane to sit in, because of the bear and everything, you know. Well, I don't know what time it was, but I thought I heard somethin' for about the tenth time. But this time it really was somethin' and not just my imagination. The damn bear is tryin' to get in the plane...he's scratchin' at the float on my side of the airplane. I'm wearin' my service revolver, a three-fifty-seven magnum, but I can't see anything. Then all of a sudden he's scratchin' around just underneath the door, dang it; but I'm not real scared or nothin', you know. I'm more worried about the paint on that new one-eighty gettin' all scratched up. Well, I figure I'll fix the rascal. I get ready with my weapon, open the door real fast, and blast him with two quick shots, and slam the door...I'm shakin' like a leaf all through it. And you know, it would turn out to be the worst part of the whole affair up to that point, because ol' Jack loved that dog more'n he cared for any human."

Joe was mortified. He could hear the black Lab yelping and squalling as he ran off into the distance. He opened the door again, not knowing what to do, it still being pitch black out there and he having no flashlight nor anything but a cigarette lighter. But then he said he saw a flashlight off in the trees a ways and could hear old Jack calling out in a quavering voice, "Did ya shoot ol' Lukey? Did ya shoot ol' Lukey?"

⁓

Joe and Jack look around in the brush with the flashlight but can't find Lukey right away. The old man is almost out of his mind with anguish and Joe is getting leery of him. Jack keeps saying over and over, "Ya shot ol' Lukey. Ya killed my dog, Joe; how come ya killed my ol' dog?"

Finally, just after daylight they find the dog. He's been hit once in the right shoulder, but he's alive. He has lost a lot of blood and is weak. They carry him over to the airplane and the old man starts getting frantic, saying they've got to get on the radio and declare an emergency, get a helicopter in there right now so they can get old Lukey to a hospital. Joe has the old man walk on down the beach unwinding the HF antennae while Joe cranks up the 180 and pretends to make some calls. "Hell," he says, "I knew there wouldn't be nobody on the radio that time of morning. Besides, I had to have time to think....Was I really going to declare an emergency—call out the Air Force, so to speak, over an injured dog?" He tells old Jack that he can't raise anybody yet and tries to buy some time till about seven when he knows that Jimmix's air taxi office in Bethel will be open. But about every thirty or forty minutes the old man insists that they try again, so they go through the same process of enactment several times. Finally, about 6:45, Joe gives a call to Jimmix and reaches him the first try. They'll be out to get him as soon as they can crank up and get off the river, he says.

༄

Jimmix gets there in a couple of hours or so, which isn't any too soon for Joe; for the last hour the old man won't even talk to him, just sits on the beach holding his dog and muttering to himself. Jimmix comes in with two Super Cubs and four guys to help labor the airplane back into the water. They decide to have one of the pilots take a plane, along with the old trapper and Lukey, and head for Anchorage. That's the biggest relief Joe experiences during the whole outing (that's what he called it, an "outing").

But the day is not over for Joe. After they get the plane back in the water, sometime in the early afternoon, Jimmix offers to fly it out. The wind has picked up some, and they've drained off some fuel. Joe says, "I had a little pride at stake here, you know, so I declined and said I'd do it myself, since I was the one that drove it in there to begin with."

So, after they've all stood around and had a smoke and talked things over, the conditions look ideal, and Joe figures he better get going before the wind changes. Once again he zigzags the plane down to the other end—he knows the boundaries of this lake fairly well by now—pours the coal to it, is up on the step by the time he reaches the point of no return where he knows he should be in the air, and although his legs and jaw are shaking from fear, he decides not to abort and begins to try to rotate the plane off the water.

But it won't come off.

By then he is no longer aware of his shaking legs jumping up and down on the rudder pedals. There's a calm that flows through him, and he is committed, like he was yesterday. But this time, he's not going to abort too late and land on the beach again, or worse, end up squashed into the five foot bank that juts up just the other side of the sandy beach. And farther on, he can see the towering birch and white spruce trees that rise in a green and golden wall—trees that are now looking taller and taller as he approaches the far end of the little lake (once again seeing in frozen image his audience, this time the new plane's nervous owner, Jimmix, off to the side, watching).

Joe breaks loose from the suction of the water, but realizes there's no way he'll clear the trees. He'll need to hold the plane near the surface within the ground effect to build some speed before he tries to pull up so he doesn't stall, but the beach and bank are already there, and he just clears the sharp bank with the fuselage...but leaves the floats behind, sheared off, while he augers the ricocheting airplane on through the brush and the waiting trees beyond—the yellow leaves and branches of autumn not so beautiful from this angle. The wings are stripped off as Joe threads the whining prop between two large birch trees and rides it out with only him and the fuselage together, slithering like an out-of-control bobsled through the leaves, frost heaves, and rocks, where they finally come to a silent standstill, not even the twittering birds wanting to believe all the racket and trashing of the countryside that they've just seen. All of it had been like a giant, runaway horse finally brought under control.

Joe says to me later, "You know, it's funny...the first thing I thought of as I climbed out through the window was, *Thank God, I don't have to worry about flyin' this thing out of here anymore.*"

CHAPTER NINETEEN

Unscheduled Pit Stop

I put my bare hand up to the defroster and jerk it back in pain, like being scalded by a boiling kettle.

In February the days get longer quickly. Now that the sun is reaching higher and the days are bright, you start to put the dark behind you. The cold is still there though. The sun at that time of year doesn't faze the deep snows, and the sun is very much aslant at its highest apex, though it now gives definition to the contours of the terrain, sharpens the shadows, and makes you think that spring is just around the corner. But it isn't. It's still three months in the future, though flying is becoming more satisfying in the cold, bright, buoyant air and longer days.

On a February day, I'm flying my state Super Cub to Anchorage from my newly assigned post at the village of Aniak on the Kuskokwim River. It's normally about a three-and-a-half hour flight. The day is typical: bright, clear, and cold; about 35 below zero on the ground. Once in the air, I climb to around 2,500 feet above the terrain, to above where the inversion line shears the sky. You can usually find the inversion, and know when you're cutting through it, from viewing the horizon as you climb out, where the far hills and mountains suddenly take on the appearance of flat-topped, southwestern mesas, and peaks are separated by thin strings from the rest of the mountain tops, creating strange configurations and mirage-like illusions.

The outside temperature is immediately warmer when you climb into the upper air, sometimes as much as thirty or forty degrees, but more often only about twenty or so degrees. This warmer air makes a difference, as you might well imagine, especially on the cockpit temperature—changing the comfort range, as is the case with me today, allowing me to remove my mittens and remain comfortable while still in my insulated flight suit, which I always wear over my uniform this time of year along with my felt-lined shoepacs.

It's all wilderness on a direct line from Aniak to Anchorage—great expanses of boreal forest, broken by white lakes and frozen rivers, with no sign of a road. In fact, all of this country that I patrol, a country about the size of Oregon, is roadless, with only an occasional village of Athabascan or Yup'ik origin dotting the landscape.

On this day, I pass over the one outpost of Hungry Village, an Athabascan community along the Stony River west of the Lime Hills. Some sixty miles beyond, I'll begin an ascent into the Alaska Range, bound for 4,000 foot Merrill Pass—a simple navigation on good weather days. Then it's a gravy descent on through the range and out along the western foothills and shoreline of Cook Inlet to Anchorage.

The calm of the cold winter days of February are conducive to smooth flight, and as I begin to fight drowsiness a couple of hours into the flight, I become uncomfortably warm. The sensation of becoming too warm can be a gradual thing, like when you're asleep and you're getting cold, but you keep lying there anyway, until it dawns on you that the furnace is out and the house is colder than the basement of a mortuary.

In this case, it's the heat; and it begins to dawn on me there's a tremendous amount of it coming out of the defroster ducts on top the instrument panel near the windscreen. Wavy fumes. At first I think it's an exceptional inversion we're in, but a check of the outside temperature gauge shows a consistent 10 degrees below zero at that altitude.

I put my bare hand up to the defroster and jerk it back in pain, like being scalded by a boiling kettle. I suck on my fingers trying to cool them, and with my left hand slide the defroster control to off. The engine sputters and almost quits. I shove the defroster back to full on, and the RPMs come back up. I don't like what I'm seeing here, not that I can see anything much. All the gauges read normal. I figure I better land right quick, and pull on carburetor heat for the descent, but the engine threatens to quit again. I leave the carb heat off, and make a power-off drop to the frozen river, where I land on the crusted snow alongside a grove of white spruce. There will be plenty of wood here if I end up spending the night, and it looks as though that might be the case as I see nothing wrong under the cowling. I'm not about to head through the Alaska Range over steep-sided, saw-toothed mountains with nowhere to land, not knowing what this overheating problem is.

On closer examination, I can see that the wooden firewall in back of the engine is beginning to take on a charred appearance behind the muffler shroud, an indication of intense heat.

This will be a cold camp over a long night, but I am thankful to be on the ground. Then, I remember a cabin not far from here. I crank up the engine, take off, and drop over onto a nearby lake where a newly-built cabin, put together by squatters, is located. It will beat Siwashing it in the spruce trees at thirty-five below zero or colder through the night. I check the firewall behind the engine of the Cub after I land. It is hot to the touch, and I reassure myself that any further flying would be foolish, if not fatal. I regret that there will be people worried about my whereabouts once my flight plan runs out. By then, it will be dark with no chance for anyone to back-fly my route until morning. Normal procedure for the FAA on overdue aircraft is to check enroute airports first via telephone, then have the Civil Air Patrol fly the route. If unable to locate the overdue aircraft, a full-blown search will be started. In the winter there is a narrow window to accomplish this due to the severity of the climate and number of hours of daylight.

I locate a key on a nail under the porch of the cabin and am preparing for a stay of at least a day or so. No sooner do I get the wood stove stoked up—the heat finally beginning to work the frost down the walls—when I hear a jet airliner crossing high in the distance. I run down to the lake, hop into the Cub, and make a blind call on 121.5, the emergency frequency. It's a Lufthansa Airlines jet heading for the Orient. They answer right away and relay my predicament and location to Anchorage Center who in turn makes a call to our Department hangar at Lake Hood.

The hangar staff dispatches one of the wildlife troopers in the Department's Cessna 185—he happened to be out in the parking lot sweeping the snow off his car at the time I called—and I'm out of there and in Anchorage within three hours of when I had been forced down. With mechanics, we repair and retrieve the airplane the next day. As it turns out, it's a rebuilt shroud around the manifold that has proven faulty. Cracked and widening, it was releasing sixteen hundred degree engine exhaust directly against the wooden firewall. It would have been only a matter of time before the plane caught fire if I had continued on.

PART FOUR:
THE ALASKA PENINSULA

*"And if thou gaze long enough into the abyss,
the abyss will soon gaze into thee."*
—Friedrich Nietzche

CHAPTER TWENTY

Wind, Rain, and Darkness

I can see the tin roof of the cabin. I know that the little landing strip is somewhere next to it, but I can't see it in the dark.

The one-man posts in the bush were the best assignments. You don't realize that when you are there, only suspicion it. Reflecting back is what clarifies it. These posts were free of distractions and petty politics.

Distractions were invented by the overwhelming state bureaucracy headquartered in the cities. The people were there to support you and your work, but they didn't know it, or had forgotten it if they ever knew it to begin with. They thought you were there to support them and their administrative and political woes. Paperwork was generated in great fits of self-importance. They knew how to cast rain on an otherwise satisfying job. But when you were out there in the country away from the telephone on important flying business, somehow that other world of offices only existed in an occasional accidental remembrance. You could deal with it when you got back in a few days…or a few weeks. No one expected to hear from you often from out in the bush. Those were the days before the world was connected by satellite.

The officer who built the outhouse, table, and chairs for the Sandy River patrol cabin was not a tall man; in fact, he stood about five-feet-four in his boots. So how could he have possibly built the furniture designed for a person of, say, six-feet-ten? Sitting on the chair, my feet barely touched the floor, and the table was about armpit high. But that wasn't the worst of it: I would have given five dollars to have had a picture of him sitting in the outhouse, with his feet lacking a yard of reaching the floor. We put up with the ill-fitting fixtures most of the season, then we took a saw and cut about six inches off the chair legs, ten inches off the table legs, and put a block of driftwood in the outhouse on which to rest one's feet.

The cabin sits on the flats alongside the clear Sandy, a river of spotted Arctic char and metallic grayling on the Bering Sea side of the Alaska Peninsula. The cabin is solidly built, and heavy cables anchor it to the ground. Only people not valuing their property fail to anchor down everything they own in this country where the winds can blow in excess of a hundred miles an hour. Occasionally, the anchoring doesn't help. One big game guide tied his Cessna 206 to two full drums of fuel. The wind picked all of it up in slow motion and laid the airplane on its back.

But, the winds in between the storms are not disturbing—winds under forty, say. You grow used to them, and they keep the bugs in hiding. They are helpful when you are tracking from the air, slowing your ground speed down to a crawl in some cases.

Two hundred feet in the air above the Bering Sea beaches is where you can find the best snooping, a notch of flaps with power honed back to 2,000 rpm. It's a smooth pace for a beachcomber, but it pays to watch ahead for someone browsing from the other direction. Two hundred feet is a well-traveled altitude for following the coast; it's like an invisible two-lane highway at certain times of the year, only there's no center line. I've had some near-misses over beaches, along rivers, and through mountain passes. Just a few. One is too many—it makes the blood jump.

Along these black beaches, the driftwood is largely spruce from out of the northern rivers: the Kvichak, Togiak, Nushagak, Goodnews, Kuskokwim, and Yukon; even some of it from the Khatyrka and Apuka rivers in Siberia. The wood is cross-hatched, stacked like blow-down at the caved-in exits of the creek mouths. And the Bering Sea looks barren in its grayness. Out from the obsidian beaches, it presents a line of travel for the Pacific walrus and gray whales up from the California currents. The whales follow the shoreline a short ways out and spout water on each rising, and you think if you dropped down just above the waves in your Super Cub, you might get a good blast, like inside a car wash, but some know better than to try it.

At Cape Seniavin, the walrus bulls haul out on the sand for a rest and soak in the sun, and you can walk amongst them—hundreds of them (the sweet stench of a hog farm attacks the nostrils). They won't spook, only grunt, as if slightly inconvenienced, and look at you walleyed, like enraged feral Hereford bulls. The walrus are 2,000 pounds each of wild, ivory-tusked, sealy beast— monolithic— with great thick bulges along their necks, like heavy warts the size of baseballs decorating the rubbery hides, and whiskers like curving monofilament ten-penny nails on their bulging, upper lips, just above the heavy ivory tusks; some of the tusks as long as three feet. The cows and bulls both have tusks. The cows' tusks are more delicate, some of them almost joining at the ends, heart-shaped.

But only the bulls haul out here. They seem benign, though, and uncaring about your presence. Skyline them, on the other hand, by coming in afoot from above on the bluffs, your silhouette against the sky, and they will panic. Trumpeting their loud, hog-like snorts, the entire herd will flounder and ripple into the sea en masse—giant yellow and tannish slugs.

༶

Here at the Sandy River patrol cabin, the day began ordinarily enough for Jim Nutgrass and me. We planned a normal patrol of fall bear hunting and guiding activities, the same routine as any of the previous twenty days or so.

If you want to know the true character of someone, camp with them for a few days. Jim and I have barely known each other previous to this assignment, and now we've been thrown into the fourth week of twenty-four-hours-a-day togetherness—just the two of us, cooking, cleaning, eating, sleeping, hauling supplies, fueling and maintaining the airplane, flying, flying, flying. Some days we can do little but lie in our bunks, listening to a seventy or eighty mile-an-hour gale trying to blow apart our plywood cabin; the oil-fueled heating stove, fire out, unable to draw and expel against the constant blast of a southwesterly blow, the soot wafting back into the tiny cabin saturating our clothes, beds, faces, hair.

I lie in the top bunk, sometimes watching the Super Cub fly on its ground-strung cables just outside the rattling window. As the wind increases, the tail lifts; then as the velocity grows in force, one wing lifts against the limber cable, then the other; and the plane flies. The plane flies toggled to the flexible cable, wheels off the ground a foot or so, suspended like an Arctic tern hovering into the wind, for what seems like hours—miles of blown sky slipping beneath the slick, fabric wings, as though it were traveling to distant places by itself. Intermittently, the wind lulls, one wheel touches, then the other. Sometimes the tail comes to rest; then the process repeats itself.

On this day the wind is soft, and we've dropped by a hunting guide's camp south of Ilnik to have a cup of coffee and shoot the bull. We've cultivated a friendship with this guide (he's one who bears watching all the time), and what better way to help keep a finger on his whereabouts and who he has in camp than to be on friendly terms and welcome in his camp?

He's gained some respect for Jim and me for a couple of reasons: One, he likes us because we're not officious and aren't too curious (at least we don't seem that way to him); and two, he respects our flying. He has always laughed at what he calls a "game warden day," a clear, blue-sky day without a cloud afloat; the only kind of day a game warden will be out and about, he says. Therefore, on the very worst days for flying—fog, blowing snow, rain squalls, no matter— we've made it a point to detour around by way of his camp and fly directly over it so he can clearly see who it is. We risk the rottenest days; we pick days when we hope it will be too foul for him to even think about untying his airplane.

We stopped by there on this day, a fair weather day to start with, and the timing couldn't have been better; he's been looking for us—there's an illegal bear hunt going on right now, he says.

One thing a guide won't tolerate, and one thing even a bandit guide will squawk about, is another guide encroaching on his guiding area, violating or not. But a violation will give him someone else to go to for handling the problem of encroachment—us. On this day, he has watched a competitor in trespass on his area drop off a hunter and assistant guide, and then chase a bear to them with his airplane. He describes the exact place of the kill, even to the precise clump of alders where the bear is down.

Jim and I fly over and locate the area. We circle the described alder patch looking for the kill. We circle and circle and search and peer until our eyeballs ache. No bear. We grow frustrated and land on a nearby patch of pumice. We're standing there talking about how we must have gotten the directions to the kill crossed up some way, when two men walk toward us from off the hill. They have come out of the very alder patch we've been circling. There's a dead bear in there too. They think we've seen them and have landed to pick them up, so they're surrendering. We play along with that idea—the idea that we are so clever and observant that while just flying by, we happen to easily spot these two men lying motionless in the tall grass beneath an entwined clump of alders, along with a bear carcass covered with grass.

One of the men admits he's the assistant guide who helped kill the illegal bear; the other is a packer. The assistant describes the illegal hunt and tells us the guide is waiting back at their camp with the hunter until the bear is skinned and packed out to the pumice patch. Jim stays to help finish skinning the bear, while I head for the guide camp.

At the camp I get a statement of admission from the out-of-state hunter. The guide won't talk to me, and leaves. It doesn't matter, we have enough. I take the hunter's rifle to use for matching up any rifle slugs found in the carcass. By the time I get back to the kill, the guide has retrieved his two helpers, and Jim is there alone with the bear hide.

It's late in the day, and I don't have room for Jim, our emergency gear, and the large bear hide all in the same load. I'll have to make a minimum of two trips before dark, and I can't leave the green bear hide, our evidence, alone. A storm is blowing in, and it may be days before I can get back. I can't leave Jim overnight for the same reason. Nor can I leave the emergency gear; it's our life insurance in case we go down in this unforgiving country.

I leave most of the emergency gear with Jim, take the bear hide, and head for camp. I get to camp, toss the bear hide out, and head back for Jim. The wind is picking up out of the southwest, and it's raining. The clouds and fog and darkness and rain are all beginning to fuse together. I barely locate Jim, but do, and we are headed back for camp. We know the country intimately after weeks of flying it in all sorts of weather, and we find our way back to the cabin like a homing pigeon. We are feeling good about that.

I can see the tin roof of the cabin, but it's like a shroud of luminescence in a vat of ink—I can't see much else. I know only that the little landing strip is somewhere next to it; the darkness and rain on the windscreen obliterate visibility, especially directly ahead.

I know also that there are five-gallon gas tins marking the ends of the short, bumpy strip, but the strip lies at a strange angle to the cabin, and the cabin is all we can find. I make a low, power-on approach, searching with my landing light for the cans, slowly weaving back and forth, Jim and I both peering into the darkness and rain, keeping up a constant chatter, as though simply having company makes circumstances seem all right, and dying less likely to happen—or maybe more acceptable. We both know that only a split second will spell the difference between spotting the cans and immediately setting the airplane down on the little strip without making the fatal mistake of landing in the hilly tundra, or slamming into the steep bank of the river, or the river itself. But we can't find our cans.

Then I spot one—a can, just ahead. I want to land, but have to force myself not to—strain my arms and fingers to obey my brain—because I need two cans to land between, otherwise I won't know which side of the can to land on, nor the proper angle for that matter.

We circle again and again, low to the ground, afraid to lose sight of the black turf with the landing light. I know we could dig a wing into the ground if not careful. (How careful can you be when you are in the middle of foolishness? I wouldn't be making steep turns this low to the ground on a clear day, under ordinary conditions, much less on a black, stormy night without a horizon to refer to.)

We're approaching a point of running out of fuel, and steep turns combined with low fuel are not compatible. The night had become, according to the French aviator Antoine De Saint-Exupery, "...an incursion into a forbidden world whence it is going to be infinitely difficult to return."

Then, Jim shouts from the back seat that there are two cans straight ahead. I peer for them, ordering my eyes to see them, keeping the power on, and dragging the plane just above the dark tundra. Then I see them as I am almost passing over, all of this within seconds—make a wrong split-second decision, and live with it forever. I chop the power, praying that the cans are not the cans on the far end of the strip, which will cause us to settle straight into the water or ram into the bank on the other side of the narrow river.

The plane bounces down the hand-cleared runway, and we roll to a stop. I shut down the engine right there. It is silent; a sudden quiet as if the heavy door to a safe were suddenly shut and you were left inside, only there is a continued low humming in the inner ear, as if the sounds of the recent flight: the pulsing, rattling Lycoming engine, the spatter of black rain, and the babbling of our loud voices, were all mixed into a singular distant sound, like a fading echo pulsing inside the head. We sit there and think about it for a long while before a word is spoken. The rain drumming on the wings is now a comfort.

CHAPTER TWENTY-ONE

Yantarni Canyon Rescue

There's a look that early-morning turbulent canyons have (you'll remember it if you've been there): dark gray-lined haze, like rich virga stringing toward the ground...

On the Pacific Ocean side of the Alaska Peninsula, the mountains slip directly into the sea. The great rock bluffs jut up like some wind-stricken Irish coastline, and an experienced pilot learns to approach that country with caution—you can get kicked around over there.

Nasty winds bellow down the coastal canyons, gales frothing the water for miles out to sea. You can view the white caps from up high as you cross the range, the quiet breezes you are riding being swallowed down through the deep canyons like the inside of a Venturi tube, the rest of the surrounding air masses hurrying to catch up, building to cyclonic forces it seems, though probably not exceeding a hundred miles an hour too often. You don't mess around in those canyons. If you land there on a quiet day, you only stay long enough to relieve yourself and go on.

The hunting guides who fly the Alaska Peninsula are familiar with the Pacific side and these windblown canyons. Knowing that, I always wondered why a particular guide decided to set up his hunting camp in the bottom of the Yantarni River canyon one year. It wasn't as though John Pangborn was new to the area, he had hunted and guided on the Peninsula for years. Maybe this was the time he decided to become better acquainted with the Pacific side. Or maybe—forgive me, John—maybe he was just stupid; he never said. In the aftermath, I only remember his face as the face of a man whose heart was beating wildly, his ample belly looking drawn a little from hunger, and a look of defeat in his frightened eyes.

We pulled him out of Yantarni in the spring after the wind blew his airplane away, scattering pieces of it down the canyon and rolling the rest into a ball; and after he, his big dog, four hunters and two assistant guides spent five or six days in a little ten-by-twelve tent in the bottom of the canyon while the wind never let up to less than around a hundred. Have you ever tried to step outside to take a whiz while the wind was blowing a steady hundred?

You might think I exaggerate, but I don't. We tried for several days to get to his camp, to no avail. We Alaska Wildlife Troopers were staying at our Pumice Creek cabin, a well-stocked patrol camp tied down with cables, over on the Bering Sea side of the Alaska Peninsula. There were four of us there, all with a state Piper Super Cub each, branching out on patrols to the far reaches of the peninsula each day, from north of Bacheroff Lake to south of the Sapsuk River country and as far as Cold Bay, but gathering back at the roost each night like chickens from out of the barnyard.

The weather was good, and had been for several days: clear skies and a fifteen to twenty knot wind out of the northwest. Excellent conditions for short takeoffs from the pumice patches where we'd been staking out troopers to catch illegal bear hunters—poachers chasing and killing brown bears with the use of airplanes. From here the terrain slopes gradually up toward the range of mountains and snowy peaks that separate the two oceans. This dusky coast is where a majority of the villages are, overlooking the shallow, gray waters of Bristol Bay and the Bering Sea.

We were staying away from the Pacific side—the canyons shrieking and sucking for air over there, the rocky coastline and deep crooked fissures churning with turbulence. Rotor clouds lay just off the summits of the peaks on the lee side—a sign which any pilot knows flashes not just major discomfort, but *danger*, like approaching a mean pit bull lying on a front porch with "Beware of Dog" signs on the gate. We were quite happy to stay off that side of the Peninsula for a while, but all good things come to an end, they say.

It was one of guide Kenny Oldham's pilots who stopped by our camp and said Pangborn was in a bind over in Yantarni, that his plane had blown away a few days ago (the last time anyone had been able to get on that side), and it looked like the tent—*a* tent—was all that was left, and no sign of anything other than pieces of his airplane scattered down the canyon.

We took off that evening in three airplanes, I guess to give each other courage, because we knew there was nothing we could do as long as the wind was up that high on the other side: Joe Brantley, Jack Allen, and I. We climbed up over those big rotor clouds that hovered off the ragged side of the range and let the wind carry us out over the Pacific Ocean beyond the rocky shores, far enough to hopefully escape the kicking turbulence. I know I didn't like it, wouldn't have done it by myself, but felt the unwarranted security of the other two planes, the other two pilots in turn either a hell of a lot braver, or more likely, just as crazy as I. Or maybe they just felt the same security, like you would if you were approaching a clump of alder where a wounded grizzly was believed to be, though likely not by yourself, but with someone else along—and even though the chances were cut in half that the bear would get you, there might be some false sense of safety. Or maybe it's like playing chicken; whoever backs out is chicken.

Anyway, we dropped below the far, downwind side of those rolling rotors, and came back up underneath them. It wasn't too bad. Then, as we neared the mouth of Yantarni, we started to get kicked around a little; and although we were cruising, we weren't making much headway. I stayed high, out of the canyon, and I don't remember where Jack was. But I remember watching Joe, down below, following the canyon up towards Pangborn's precarious camp.

I was bouncing along, not gaining much over the ground far below, the three of us keeping up a chatter on the radio, and eventually I could see that Joe wasn't going anywhere at all, his plane just standing stationary against the wind. Now and then he would move to one side or the other like you've seen a fish maneuver against the current of a swift brook—first this way and then that way, but not moving forward, and although the trout looks like he's resting, he has to be swimming at least as fast as the current in order to stay in one spot in relation to the stream bed. I asked Joe how fast he was indicating, and he said a hundred or a little over, and that the air was smooth, oddly enough. He said he wasn't getting anywhere at all. I said I could see that, and told him, "You better get the hell out of there, Joe."

It must have bothered me a little that he didn't answer me and that I could see him still playing with the current. So I said something else, not printable but profound; and Jack, who we both respected when it came to flying, said something sage about then like, "Joe, get your Irish ass out of there!"

Be that as it may, someone yelled *chicken*, and little Joe backed out. We climbed and sailed away like kiting swifts fleeing down the wind; up and out toward Yantarni Bay and the churning Pacific beyond; over the deep, green water as though it conjured up something safe in the mind. Poised like Icarus above the Aegean Sea; a cold, unforgiving, wind-swept ocean—far away from boats and helicopters and rescue services—but wide open water that seemed okay because it was away from the wild canyons.

And what if you did suck a piston out there and go down in the drink? Your fellow officers would circle and watch you die, and you might even wave at them, after you crawled out on a sinking wing. They would waggle their wings in some sort of final salute, because they would know there was nothing they could do. Though that might sound melodramatic, try flying out there sometime—those thoughts will be real to you too. It's your way of coping with the fear, like a soldier not wanting to die, but if he must, then he would like to die like a man, but not alone. Only what could be more alone than dying?

But here and now the real problem is how do we get guide John Pangborn out of Yantarni canyon? We head back to our camp at Pumice Creek and don't talk about it much to each other over the radio. Once we're in the clear, meaning over the top of the rotors and heading back across the peaks to the pumice patches on the Bering Sea side, we even quit whatever little chattering we're doing and are left deep within our own thoughts, each trying to come up with a solution.

It seemed to me that this was getting to be a serious matter: Pangborn's got some hunters down there—we don't know how many then—and they are probably suffering within our sight. We've seen the tent on the gray gravel of the braided river, but there's no sign of life. How would you hear anything if you were down there with the wind hallowing your tent, trying to uproot it? After all, it wouldn't be like trying to listen above the sounds of a poker game in session. After a week, you and the assistant guides and hunters who trusted you to take them into a safe environment wouldn't be talking much. And if the hunters were talking at all, it wouldn't be to you. Isn't that right, John? You never even said thanks after this was all over, did you, John. Well, I guess that's alright. We did what we had to do; didn't do it for the thanks. And I guess maybe you didn't want to draw any more attention to your embarrassment by saying a simple thank you. I don't believe there was a one of us thought about the thanks then, certainly not little Joe. I never heard him say anything. For all I know, maybe you told him thanks before he died a while after that—the pain of cancer in his bones. He never thought about himself, didn't make a big to-do about saving people. Guess he figured it would all come out in the wash. Maybe this is the wash, John.

Well, anyway...that night we decide the next morning is going to be a have-to thing. We'll take all our resources, four planes, and head out very early while the winds are at their lowest, and try this thing again.

⁂

Before daylight we take off—we've added Wildlife Trooper Garland Dobson to our squadron—and by dawn we are topping the bleak spine of the range, looking into the deep abysses of the blustery, black southern canyons. There's a look that early-morning turbulent canyons have (You'll remember it if you've been there.): dark, gray-lined haze, like rich virga stringing toward the ground, but unanchored to the clouds or even to the unstable air in its raggedness. And always, the rotor clouds hanging above like stationary turmoil—the only sky-borne things still attached to roots.

We can see beyond, out to the Pacific Ocean, but the water isn't frothing so much now in the dark morning dim. We chatter on the radio. Someone sees a light down the canyon coming in from the Pacific. A boat light out in the bay or what? It's hunting guide Kenny Oldham. There are two more lights—they're landing lights in the sky, not mast lights on the sea—Oldham and a couple of his pilots. Now there are seven of us, all Super Cubs. We make contact with Oldham on the emergency frequency and develop a plan. We'll each take an individual—land one at a time and take one out till we've got them all, however many there are. Kenny says he'll go first. We're lining our way up the canyon, like headlights on an interstate, just at daylight. The wind is laying down some, blowing maybe forty with higher gusts at John's camp, enough to lift away a Super Cub sitting on the ground untied. Can God find us out here—watch over us this far away?

Kenny takes two people on his stop. He says it's squirrelly, not good; better make hay while the sun shines, he says, stay with the airplane...fly it while you're waiting for someone to climb in...fly it on the ground—keep it from getting away...keep the wind from sailing it away like an errant kite. But I can see little Joe, walking around outside his plane in his wing-tipped brogans. I'm making my approach slowly, like a mallard in slow motion, cupped wings into the wind; and Joe is there at the camp, walking around like he just stopped in for a visit and a cup of coffee, maybe wants to know how everything is going, "How's it goin'?" His plane is hopping around like it wants to fly away. The little, weak brakes are set, but they won't hold long, I figure. *Joe, get in the airplane, put someone in there with you, and get out of there. We need some room!* He does, finally.

This narrow part of the canyon sits downstream from a big bend in the valley. At the bend there is a cliff, a sheer bluff where the wind is boiling over before it funnels down through the canyon. To do this thing right, you need to take off, gain some altitude and airspeed, then gently try to bank downwind, and still leave yourself room for the turn in the narrow canyon. But if you go too far up the canyon before you start the turn, you're going to get into that burble off the bluff—just like water rolling over a boulder. (It's the best way to think of the wind when you fly the mountains: think of it as a river flowing; the currents will be the same.)

I'm next to last to land. Only Pangborn and his German Shepherd are left. John loads his frightened dog into the baggage compartment behind the rear seat of my Cub and climbs in himself, while I ride the controls, following the gusts and currents on the ground. Dobson lands behind me—he won't even get to take the dog—and says later that as I take off, climbing almost immediately without a forward run, my Cub rolls onto its side, the wing missing the ground by maybe four inches. I remember something about it, remember my right hand full of wavering wings and wild ailerons, jamming the stick to the left so far I have to lift my leg almost off the rudder pedal to allow full aileron. I head for the bluff, get some altitude before turning, then easy does it; allow that airspeed to catch up; too steep in the turn and it'll stall. It's carrying us sideways now and we're moving toward the side of the canyon walls, but it's okay. We build up some more speed before making the final turn, then we're headed downwind, doing over a hundred where a few seconds ago the speed of the airplane over the ground was, at best, ten miles an hour; and now we're climbing out down the canyon, John Pangborn and his old dog all grins and slobbers.

CHAPTER TWENTY-TWO

Sandy River Mother's Day

I could see Roy...I could see the surface of the water just inches above my face. I was straining, but I couldn't get there.

This particular spring day on the Alaska Peninsula dawns clear and calm—an event which causes pilots to constantly eye the horizon with distrust. When the wind stops, you take notice. The quiet is abrupt, like a forewarning of something ominous on the horizon.

It is the spring of 1982 when Wildlife Troopers Garland Dobson and Roy Breckinridge are flying a patrol of the brown bear hunting season and are staying at the Pumice Creek patrol cabin, using it as a base camp. They occasionally stay overnight wherever it catches their fancy, their camp gear stashed in the baggage compartment and tied to the wing struts of the unmarked state Super Cub Garland is flying. They are posing as bear hunters.

As can be expected, the calm lasts but a few hours, and a big wind blows in from the southeast. Garland notices some of the wind and turbulence kicking up as they fly past Wild Man Lake, southwest of Port Heiden. That might have been a good sign to just stay over at the Sandy River cabin, down near the coast and not far from where they are, but they are scheduled to meet some other troopers across the mountains on the Pacific Ocean side. By the time they are far up the Sandy River valley, well into the range of mountains that divide the peninsula, Garland decides it's much too turbulent to fly through the passes, so he lands at a guide camp there in the canyon to bide some time. As it turns out, there isn't anyone at home, so rather than get knocked around anymore, they decide to stay over.

It isn't much of a camp, according to Garland, "Just a bare-bones shack with tin for the sides, and big gaps in the corners."

There are a couple of bunks, but no stove. "Well, there was a stove," he says, "but it didn't work…it was an oil stove without any oil, and there wasn't any stovepipe."

With the Super Cub tied down, and the wind developing into a gale, they turn in to listen to the whistling of the empty stove pipe hole. It is a Friday. The wind picks up to over seventy miles per hour that night.

Saturday comes. And Saturday night. The wind is the same. Garland worries that the buried logs the wings are tied to are going to be pulled out of the ground. They hold, but the plane is rocking and jumping at the ropes day and night. By Sunday noon, after telling and re-telling every yarn they can think of for the last forty-eight hours, Garland and Roy notice the wind has eased to about twenty. It's time to make a break.

While doing his pre-flight of the Cub, Garland notices that the tie-down ring at the top of the left strut is bent. He tugs at it to see if it's loose. It appears solid. He takes a closer look by cutting away some of the fabric with his knife and sees that a piece of channeling is bent up inside there, but it still looks structurally sound to him. He and Roy load up and take off upriver from the little gravel bar that serves as an airstrip.

Just as they are airborne and out over the swift running river, they hear a snap. "We were about a hundred and fifty feet in the air when I heard the snap," Garland says, "It was the front strut, and the leading edge of the wing came up. The plane started to roll, and I headed for a swampy area figuring it'd be softer there. Then the rear strut snapped, and that's all she wrote…the whole wing just went. I yelled out to Roy, in the back seat, 'Hang on!' I remember thinking, *This is gonna be bad*."

The plane drops out of the air and hits the river inverted. The river is swift and about three feet deep, but Garland says he isn't worried right then. He says, "I just felt cocky for still being alive."

The next thing Garland knows, he's fighting for air from underneath the freezing May snow melt. He says he almost panics, then realizes he hasn't unfastened his seat belt. He jerks it loose and again tries to get out, but he can't. The engine has been jammed back into the cockpit, and he can't move—he can't breathe.

It is Mother's Day.

"I thought about my wife and kids, and that I wasn't gonna see 'em anymore," he says, "and I was thinkin', *What a hell of a Mother's Day present.*"

He finally decides he is going to have to "gulp water" when he feels someone pulling him by the hair. It's Roy. Although Roy is also pinned in, he has somehow managed to get his head and one arm and shoulder out of the water, and in that position, oblivious to anything else, is trying to pull Garland up. But, the slightly built trooper cannot pull his husky partner up far enough.

Garland says, "I could see Roy...I could see the surface of the water just inches above my face. I was straining, but I couldn't get there. It was crazy," he says, "I remember thinking at the time about this movie I'd seen once—this guy drowned the same way—and I knew I was gonna drown, and I'm thinkin' about this movie, and Roy is staring me in the face, pulling on me."

Somehow, with super-human effort, Roy pulls Garland's face to the surface, just enough "for half a choking breath of part air and part water." It is enough air for that extra effort that Garland needs, and he is suddenly free and standing in waist-deep water.

Now it's Garland's turn to help. He tries to pull Roy out of the wreckage, but Roy's foot is hung up in the controls. Once again, Garland doesn't panic. He works his way back under the swift water into the cramped wreckage, locates the tangled foot, and works it loose. They are both free.

Hypothermia is now the biggest enemy. Roy can barely walk. The upper part of his pelvic bone is chipped, as it turns out, and he is in pain. He can't put his weight on his right leg. They are across the fifty-foot-wide, waist-deep river from the cabin. They are soaked through, and the wind is still up to about fifteen mph. The ambient temperature is in the mid-thirties, the chill much worse.

With Roy hanging onto his partner, and with only one foot to use as a brace against the current, they pick their way across the swift river, over the slick rocks to the other shore. Then Garland goes back across to try to get their gear out of the plane. He is able to get the two Army surplus mummy bags and his emergency pack out. When he gets back across the river, Roy has already done a one-legged hop to the cabin about seventy-five yards away.

They know their problems aren't over. They are wet and freezing, camped in an airy shack without a stove, with only two soggy down sleeping bags, and not knowing when anyone will show up.

Roy is in the worst shape. He is suffering from hypothermia, his lips are blue, and he is mumbling incoherently. "I figured my fat was all that was saving me," Garland says, "but Roy is as skinny as a rail, not an ounce of fat on him."

Although he is sure there is nothing of use in the shack, Garland finds "two old cheap bedrolls full of shrew crap" in a box against the wall. "The kind of bedrolls you see at the dime store," he says.

Cheap and full of shrew droppings maybe, but dry.

He gets Roy out of his wet clothes and into both bags. Then he brings out his small alcohol stove, but his disposable lighter will not work. However, he finally gets the stove fired up by using his magnesium bar, and makes some hot chocolate. Roy is still mumbling, and says he won't drink it. "I don't want it," he says, and coughs most of it up when Garland insists.

Garland says the cold has started to really work on him by now. He hasn't noticed it so much before. When Roy begins to look and act somewhat normal, Garland takes one of the sleeping bags and gets in. "Then," he says, "Roy spent the rest of the night hollering at me every fifteen minutes, making sure I was OK."

There hadn't been anyone in the area yet that spring, but the guide who owns the camp, Jeff Graham, flies in that next afternoon along with a German hunter who gives them dry clothes from out of his own duffle. Later, Graham flies Dobson to Port Heiden, where by telephone he is fortunate enough to locate a Coast Guard helicopter from Kodiak on the ground at King Salmon. They fly down to retrieve both Roy and Garland.

CHAPTER TWENTY-THREE

Bad Bob and His Flying Machines

The monotonous drone of an engine—in comforting cadence with your heartbeat when you're out over water or above the overcast—can awaken you to stark fear when it sputters to dead silence.

It is in the fall of the year, somewhere north of Becharof Lake, when Wildlife Trooper Dick Dykema flies over Bandit Bob as he is pouring a five gallon can of gasoline on his own airplane.

Dick circles and watches Bob trail the aviation gas out away from the Super Cub. Bob keeps turning his head away from the circling airplane, hiding his face. But after chasing Bandit Bob for years, Dick figures he would know old Bob even in the dark. When he still refuses to look up, Dick drops down low, cuts the throttle, opens the side window of his Cub, and hollers, "Hi, Bob, how you doin'?"

Startled, Bob looks up, then giving a little wave, steps over and lights a match to the fuel he has trailed away from the plane. The whole thing goes up in a ball of flame. Bob stands there, now defiantly shaking his fist at Dick, while Dick circles, transfixed, disbelieving. Bob's client, a German hunter, stands off to one side, no doubt convinced that he has made a poor choice this year in a hunting guide, and no doubt afraid of what this crazy American is going to do next. The German says later that Bob had a fit when he saw the game warden's plane appear; that Bob rolled on the ground, and that he "ate the dirt in big bites."

The hunter need not have been afraid. It was just Bob's style. Get caught in the act of illegally killing a bull moose by use of an airplane? Just burn the airplane to keep the state from getting it. We had already taken a couple of his airplanes over the past few years, and there would be another one or two later. Where Bob came up with the money for these airplanes, I have no idea. As far as eating the dirt, well, what can I say? While awaiting his hour in court, Bob scribbled something on a piece of paper and left it on Dick's desk in our office in King Salmon. It said, "In every silver lining there's a black cloud."

As long as Bandit Bob was still alive, he was out there somewhere killing something—or stealing something. A few years before the dirt-eating episode, when I was stationed at McGrath, I went out one morning to discover that the extension cord and emergency locator beacon had been taken out of my state Super Cub. Three other cords and another beacon were missing from other airplanes in town. A snowstorm during the night had wiped out any tracks from around the airplanes. I figured the thief was one of the local kids—even had a good idea who. I had not realized that Bandit Bob had been in town that night, nor was I aware that he had failed to pay the bill for himself and two of his hunters at the McGrath Roadhouse when he left. I don't recall if it was hunting season or not. But it makes no difference. Bob hunted all year.

Not long after that, a fellow officer called from the Anchorage office. They had found my locator beacon in Bandit Bob's airplane, hidden behind the baggage compartment of his Super Cub. It seems Bob had killed a grizzly bear out of season, and when he went back to retrieve the hide, a wildlife officer, who was staked out in the snow, popped out of the brush and nabbed him, seizing his plane. I forget which of his Super Cubs that was, but anyway, there was my beacon, the state inventory number scratched on the bottom.

Then a big lodge out on the Susitna River, closed up for the winter, was burglarized of all the mounted trophy animal heads and hides, scores of them. Where were they recovered? In Bandit Bob's attic near Chugiak.

The interesting thing was, Bob was such a likeable person. You couldn't help but like him. To meet him you would think, *Now there's a nice guy.*

I don't know if Bob was lucky or unlucky. He was caught so many times that you might say he was unlucky, but how he could stay out of jail for most of his life was pure luck. I think the judges just felt sorry for him; he had such a hangdog look.

An example of his bad-luck/good-luck was the time he decided to fly from the island of Kodiak across the open sea to the mainland of the Kenai Peninsula in a single-engine airplane on wheels. I believe his young daughter was with him. The weather was bad, so Bob just climbed up on top of the rotten weather, above the clouds, and kept going. The engine quit on him somewhere out over the water while still above the clouds. That was the bad luck. You've heard of a snowball's chance in hell—well, that's what chance Bob had of getting out of that situation alive. The monotonous drone of an engine—in comforting cadence with your heartbeat when you're out over water or above the overcast—can awaken you to stark fear when it sputters to dead silence, and the prop slowly windmills, or freezes as an inanimate object in front of the windscreen. But as Bob glided down out of the clouds, he found a fishing boat right there, the only one for many miles. Bob just put the plane in the drink and was promptly fished out.

Bob was a killer of animals. Above everything else he did, he loved to kill. This is not a common thing. The majority of hunters don't go out in the woods for that single purpose of mind (even though their wives might think so). It is not a mania with them to kill. I've known only a few people like that, and Bandit Bob was the worst. For these few like Bob, it didn't matter if they had a hunting partner; they didn't care about the companionship, nor the outdoor experience. Like a sociopath, the manic killer kills for the killing.

I suppose this sort of person may have been looked upon with reverence in the old days. He would have been constantly hunting and killing and bringing in meat for the entire village. But he would be an aberration today. Bandit Bob was an aberration. We finally grew tired of catching him; there comes a point at which you have to spread some of the budget around to others. Bob was later killed while trying to fly through a blinding snowstorm. Unfortunately, he took his good wife with him.

༺࿐༻

I've been a hunter most of my days, and been around them all my life. I know all of their stories and jokes and know most of their thoughts. It's like kids out on the playground: You watch them and they sound the same as the kids when you were young and out there; in fact, you can pretty well tell what they're thinking and what they're going to do next. It is that sort of thing with me and hunters.

Hunters are predictable. At least they are predictable somewhat like automobile drivers are predictable. Drivers get behind the wheel—it doesn't matter what their status or profession is in real life—they get in the driver's seat and assume another personae, often becoming clones of what they believe a driver ought to be.

That's the way it is with hunters. You meet them in the field and you have no way of knowing what their occupations are; they've reverted to being hunters—good, bad, or otherwise. Now, don't take this as a sign of bitterness with me, but I've never seen any activities in which ordinarily honest people are more tempted to lie, cheat, and steal than I've seen with hunters and fishermen. But like an old-time game warden told me, "Remember, they ain't all bad, so treat 'em with respect; it might be the only time they meet a game warden. But watch out, every hunter ain't a sonofabitch, but every sonofabitch goes huntin'."

~

The genetic impulse to hunt builds up in the urban man. It becomes a frantic thing when the limited hunting season, say, for deer, approaches. Something within tells him he is still a stealthy stalker of food sources. He abandons his couch, the city, and the pavement for the inclimate woods where he expects to feel comfortable. He has time off from work, or maybe just a weekend. It is a concerted squeezing of his nomadic hunter's juices into one short span of time. No wonder he and his cohorts often become a menace to the highways, to the woods, to each other.

But a hunter who has the chance to go out often into the woods usually becomes more relaxed with the surroundings. He may even find that he spends much of his time just relishing the open air and the countryside, and doesn't wish to kill anything. He may eventually find that he spends time engrossed in studying and contemplating his favorite haunts more closely—feeling a reverence, in fact. For him, maybe the need to hunt is really just a sideline needed to come back to a natural environment; he has not been removed from it for so very long. There are comforts there he sometimes no longer understands.

There's a great thrill to the hunt, the chase. It's not a small item to be raised a hunter. The young hunter is given to expect a challenge. He is prepared to pit himself against hardships in the field and the intelligence of an animal. He is entrusted to make good his promise of success, and whether he is able to carry that out, including properly handling the killing, the butchering, and the removal of the prey from the field, or not, is a matter of pride. Once he has decided he is a hunter, once he has made that commitment, he is destined to be successful in the hunt. Anything less may be considered a failure. And if he is lucky in his effort, then there is elation—an acceptance into the fraternity. And if he is a member of a purely bareboned, aboriginal tribe deep within the Amazonian watersheds, it is natural. But if he is a member of modern society, maybe it no longer is so. And maybe he decides he needs to think about it.

CHAPTER TWENTY-FOUR

The Sting

He sits in the cockpit threatening to start the engine while one of the troopers stands under the prop.

The guide and his client crouch in a patch of snow as the big grizzly surges up the hill toward them, trashing the willows, scattering the snow, and blowing slobbers. The gap is narrowed to less than a hundred yards.

"Don't shoot till I tell you to," the guide says, "and when you shoot, place your shot into the shoulder. We need to break him down."

The hunter settles the cross-hairs of his scope unwaveringly centered on the loping bear, his heart pounding in his throat.

But this is not a charging bear; this bear has not even seen the men. He is a bear running for his life from a Piper Super Cub persistently boring in from behind, blasting him with its whining prop and backfiring Lycoming engine all the way up the hill from the frozen creek bottom, where he was rudely flushed from his bed.

"Shoot him now," the guide says, as the panting, slobbering, bruin angles toward the two men, now within sixty yards. The hunter complies, dropping the bear with one shot. In a snarling, fit-throwing rage, the grizzly bites at the pain as though it were a stinging insect. But he is unable to scare it away, and he finally succumbs to the overwhelming power of it all, breathing his last in the fading snow patches of late spring.

"Put another one in him for good measure," the guide says, while the chase plane flies off to land on a faraway ridge. Then the guide, well-practiced, begins to quickly skin the large bear. The client casually snaps pictures of the bear and the guide, also taking overlapping panoramic photos of the surrounding horizon. Then he surreptitiously hangs a small, dull object behind a willow branch nearby. It is a homing device. I will take it off the branch myself in a few days.

The client is Nando Mauldin, an undercover U.S. Fish and Wildlife Service agent, at that time based in Washington, D.C. as head of Special Operations. The shooting of this bear is the event that will break the back of an illegal guiding operation which has plagued western Alaska for years.

☙

It isn't easy to outsmart a man at his own business if he is successful in that business, and we had some successful bandit guides in the old days. These fellows used airplanes illegally and were adept at it. To get into their heads we had to understand exactly how they worked. It was not conceivable to a non-flyer that a guide/pilot could pull off the antics that he often did, nor was it conceivable to the average flying hunter or even wildlife officer. The challenge presented to us was simple actually: learn what they were doing, how they were doing it, and then stop them. Is it possible to outsmart a fox at his livelihood? Well, sure, trappers do it all the time. We needed to be trappers.

Supply and demand. And greed. Over the years several Alaska hunting guides have succumbed to the pressure of an unhappy hunter who has failed to bag the animal he has come to Alaska for. The guide feels the need to produce—and if the price is right, some will be tempted to illegally produce. Taking game with the help of an airplane becomes the easy way out, and what better way to select the best animal out of thousands of square miles of country in one day? Why spend days and days scouring a few square miles of country by foot, with only one or two hunters, and no guarantee of a kill? A one-day airplane hunt can produce the best of several bears that are spotted, and the hunter can enjoy the special comforts of a lodge at the end of the day. In this manner, a heap of bears can be taken during a short season that is only open for fifteen days. The hunter is thus robbed of the defining moment of taking a once-in-a-lifetime brown/grizzly bear: That defining moment is the hunt itself—a fair chase hunt.

We game wardens had been stymied for years in trying to stop this activity. Up until 1972, an indifferent Fish and Game Department hierarchy, for whom our enforcement division worked at that time, would not listen to our pleas for more productive enforcement techniques. When asked for support to use some undercover hunters in 1970, the reply of the Fish and Game Commissioner to a small group of us at a meeting in Fairbanks was, "We're not playing that cloak and dagger shit."

So the bandit guides—I prefer to separate them from the legitimate guides by that designation—continued to have their field day with Alaska's big game. It meant big money for them. Simple arithmetic: more bears, more money.

We were ineffective, to a great degree, in those days while with the Alaska Fish and Game Department, and a joke to many of the big-time bandits. We continued to bring most of our cases and arrests against the general hunting public, while the bandit guides seemed to be untouchable. Catching one in the act was next to impossible without the support of our agency.

Then a fortunate thing happens. In 1972, April to be exact, the Governor of Alaska, Bill Egan, becomes angered with our enforcement division over pay squabbles. He considers the division a "loose cannon," and through the power of his office, simply gives us the choice of moving, lock-stock-and-barrel, over to the State Troopers, or being fired—the lot of us. It is the biggest favor he can do for us, and for wildlife protection (although he was not thinking of the wildlife when he did it). We are finally where we belong: in an organization where the priority is professional law enforcement and the politics are minimal.

Within two years, after the initial transition miseries that accompany moving a whole division in with another, we have the support and money we need for undercover operations.

Meanwhile, I've been asked by the Commissioner of Public Safety to move into Anchorage, a big city by Alaska standards. Once again I'm giving up the outdoors for the desk, fighting rush-hour traffic to and from work, facing four walls that can close in if I let them. But I don't. I break away into the bush as much as possible to keep the cobwebs out of my gut. Then, after a year and a half as detachment commander, I am pushed up to head sport fish, game, and guide enforcement statewide.

In this new position I am given the authority to initiate a covert agreement with the U.S. Fish and Wildlife Service, working through Special Agent in Charge of Alaska Ray Tremblay. The Service has recently been funded a special section for nationwide undercover operations, and already has a few well-trained, experienced officers established as undercover agents in various sections of the country. One of these is Nando Mauldin, whom I worked with when we were both officers in the New Mexico Game and Fish Department. After twenty years with New Mexico, he has gone to work for the feds.

The work in setting up some hunts begins. No smart bandit guide is going to book a hunter he is suspicious of, and the really prolific ones already have plenty of bookings. Why take on an unknown, un-referenced client? Most of the guides run background checks on prospective clients, and some of them later wished they had done a better job of it.

Jim Nutgrass, eventually in charge of the state Fish and Wildlife Investigations Section, takes over the state end of the preparations, and through a couple of years of hard work with the federal undercover section, connects on some initial bookings. Two of these bandits, who work as partners, will have Nando Mauldin as their client.

˜

These two guides have been taking twelve to fifteen bears in a fifteen-day hunting season and have been doing it year after year. There is no legitimate way they can take that many bears and stay within the law. They have to be taking them by direct use of their aircraft. Laws have been enacted to prevent this "unfair chase" by making it unlawful to take a bear on the same day a hunter has been airborne. In addition, it is in violation of state and federal laws to harass wildlife with an aircraft.

We have been staking out guides suspected of this sort of activity, watching their camps and lodges, recording the comings and goings, trying to match hunters leaving in the morning with those returning with freshly killed bears in the evening. We are not often successful. The guides simply set up a spike camp after taking a bear, overnight the hunter and assistant guide, and pick them up the next day.

A law is enacted requiring the registration of a specified number of camps a guide can maintain. Bear hides cannot be transported except from these designated camps to designated airports, and guided hunters cannot hunt from other than registered camps. The bandit guides work around this; they fly the hunters into the registered camps after making the kill. The only chance they take is being seen letting the hunter and assistant out of the airplane near where a bear is spotted, then driving the bear to them.

We can't stake out every hunting camp in the country. Nor can we monitor the thousands of square miles of bear habitat. But we can locate

The Sting

the best areas of bear concentration and send in a stakeout officer with a camouflaged camp to be on the watch. On occasion this works, but it has not worked in capturing Nando's two guides. However, on this hunt—the hunt that nails them—we have our blood brother in their midst.

Nando is prepared for at least a few days of some semblance of hunting. Even he would not have believed the sequence of events if he had not been there to watch them unfold.

He is picked up by one of the guides in Anchorage with a Cessna 185 and flown several hundred miles out to the lodge, beyond the Alaska Range near the village of Nondalton on Lake Clark. They overnight there, awaiting the arrival of the other guide and two more hunters. Over dinner and drinks that night, Nando volunteers to delay his hunt so that the other hunters, two doctors from Los Angeles, can hunt first. This allows Nando to remain in a position to document enough evidence about the doctors' hunts to later use in bringing a case against the guides if the hunts are successful. The doctors have their bears within two days.

The next day it's Nando's turn. He and the two guides take off in a couple of Piper Super Cubs and fly a beeline 130 miles to the west, into the headwaters of the Holitna River, completely out of the area the guides normally hunt. Good bears are getting harder to find closer to the lodge. It is difficult for Nando to keep track of where they are in the hundreds of square miles of wilderness, none of which he has ever been in. He cannot afford to appear too interested in their whereabouts, but he knows he will need to remember where they've been. Sitting directly behind the pilot, he can keep small notes on the inside of a matchbook cover as to the magnetic headings and the time traveled. They eventually land on a hilltop, where a tent is set up housing two sets of airplane skis, a small amount of camping gear, and extra aviation fuel. The planes are taxied to the edge of the snow, where the guides remove the tundra-tired wheels from both airplanes, replacing them with skis. They refuel and take off—two guides, two airplanes, and one hunter—to scour the treeless hills beyond the Kogrukluk River.

"We located several bears," Nando says later, "and circled them to determine the size and condition of the pelts. One was a large, blond boar, who reared up on his back legs and ran, reaching for our airplane as we flew just overhead. The guide said he wasn't big enough."

In a short while they locate the hapless, chocolate-colored grizzly in a creek bottom. The guide says to Nando, "That is your bear." The scene is set for a quick kill, the two bandits discussing the plan of attack over their radios.

"When we landed," Nando says, "we used every foot of the little patch of snow, sliding right up to within a few feet of the end of it."

Nando is careful not to make suggestions at any point regarding the hunt, to simply allow the guide to instruct him on taking the bear in the manner of their normal procedures. "I felt somewhat dirty," he says later, "for having to kill such a fine animal to get at individuals profiting at the expense of the resource."

After skinning the bear, the guide takes off with the hide, meeting the other airplane several miles away to exchange the cargo. Nando is left with only his rifle and camera. At that point he has a twinge of concern that if he is suspected of being an undercover officer, he might well be left where he stands. He puts the thought out of his mind and busies himself taking more photos of the scene. When the guide returns for him, a reverse of the morning flight takes place: back to the tent on the ridge, change the skis to wheels, and back to the lodge, far to the southeast.

All in one day.

A nice, cozy wilderness bear hunt; a nice, cozy profit. Three trophy bears in three days. Make ready for more hunters! But the profit is destined to be somewhat restricted for these two guides.

∽

There are reports to complete, complaints to file, arrest warrants and seizure warrants to serve, interviews to conduct. Emotions run high. One of the two guides threatens to run over the troopers and agents with the airplane they've come to seize at Merrill Field in Anchorage—the Cessna 185, which was used to transport the illegally taken bear hides. He sits in the cockpit, threatening to start the engine while one of the troopers, little Joe Brantley, who the guide knows and respects, stands under the prop. Will he start the engine? There is a limit to what this particular guide will stoop to. He has reached his limit in this case. The two Super Cubs used to take the bear are also seized.

Several days go by before Investigator Jack Jordan and I can head out to investigate the crime scene, a necessary step in corroborating Nando's statements. We have a tracking device on the Super Cub I am flying, and a fairly good idea of the general area of the kill, thanks to Nando's observations, and his panoramic photos of the country around the kill scene.

There is only one problem (but it has been anticipated): What snow there was is almost gone, and I will have to locate an area to land on wheels, preferably close by. It takes us a while to locate the kill. There is a ridge above it that looks landable, but I use up some valuable fuel in looking it over carefully. My concern is not so much the landing, as it is the takeoff after we get on the ground. The wind is ideal for landing, coming straight down the ridge. But because it is rather steep, the takeoff will have to be downhill, unfortunately also downwind. Under certain light wind conditions, this can work out, but conditions are not that way today. I know that the afternoon or late evening winds generally switch to moving up the canyons. It is with this in mind that I finally commit us to landing.

We take duplicate photos of Nando's panorama and the bear carcass, gather an empty shell casing, locate a bullet by aid of a metal detector—it entered the bear and traveled several yards up the inside of an intestine before coming to rest—and retrieve the homing device from the bush where Nando left it. We have plenty of time; the wind has not switched for a favorable takeoff. By late afternoon, however, the wind dies down and we make it off the ridge in one full-throttled, galloping piece.

෴

The two guides have a lot at stake, but so do we. If this case does not finish them, we are out of any more good ideas, I think. They hire a battery of attorneys to sift and chew their way through the state and federal charges and evidence. But it is a tight case.

Meanwhile, the feds get information that there are death threats being made, that a contract is out for Nando. A source is traced back to Detroit, to an organized crime family hit man. Nando is ordered to leave the D.C. area and assume a new identity until the long court battles are over. At one of the hearings in Alaska, a defense attorney seeks to gain favor with the judge by pointing out that Nando is apparently armed while testifying and that there "are sixteen armed guards in the courtroom, your honor, and how is my client supposed to get a fair hearing!"

"There have been so many death threats over this case that even I am armed," the judge says. "I don't think the fact that the witness is armed will affect his ability to tell the truth...I suggest if you have further questions for this witness, you proceed with them."

The two guides are convicted. They serve jail time, lose three airplanes, are assessed a sizeable fine, and lose their guide licenses and exclusive guide areas.

We are in business! The rest of the bandit guides can either straighten up their act or start running scared, as far as I'm concerned. Some of the borderline bandits will switch back to more legitimate operations; not many of them can afford taking chances.

Others had not yet learned.

CHAPTER TWENTY-FIVE

Wilderness Stakeouts

*Maybe he became at ease with me because he figured
I was not smart enough to catch him. I did not need to
be—he was smart enough for both of us.*

We had several troopers whose attributes fit the category for stakeout duty for bandit guides: woods savvy, trained, and well-experienced law enforcement officers who would not screw up a crime scene, an interview, or an arrest; yet, officers who were fearless and smart when they were in the haunts of the brown/grizzly bear.

It took quite some time to find these men within the ranks of over 300 Alaska State Troopers. We asked for volunteers and had plenty of them, but we only had their say-so as to their ability to take care of themselves, be observant, and cope with the stresses of total solitude and aggressive bears. One stakeout, who had smuggled a few gallons of hard booze in with his gear, drank himself drunk every day. Not only was he removed from stakeout duty, he was removed from the state payroll. Another literally begged off after being out alone only three days. In time we finally had a handful of "specialists," and another handful of pilot/troopers skilled at getting these stakeouts safely in and out of tight places. These were all wildlife troopers—few of the road troopers were qualified, although they liked the idea of getting paid to "camp."

I was put in charge of training these stakeouts, buying their gear, and picking their assignments. A team of ten stakeouts and ten pilots (with short field and rough terrain flying capabilities) was hand-picked and furnished with the very best in equipment and survival gear. The stakeouts were given cold-weather and other survival training at Eielson Air Force Base near Fairbanks, and in addition, as time allowed, each were sent to work for a season with an active big game guide to better understand the guiding industry.

We had more bandit guides to catch. The two we had captured with Nando's help were not the only ones out there. Another one in particular had needed catching for a long time. For years he had been a carnivorous Pac Man on the Alaska Peninsula brown bear population. He had become the proprietor of a killing machine—a Quik Stop for lazy hunters.

But he was smart and learned by others' mistakes. No undercover hunt had been set up with him as he screened his hunters closely and chose carefully. We captured a few of the younger guides he had trained as they branched out on their own to make their fortunes. I watched some of them emulate their mentor almost to perfection, but they lacked his intelligence. You had to admire his industriousness and his aggressiveness.

I liked this man once I got to know him. You cannot hate a man for what he does and be smart about capturing him. If I saw him on the street today, I would be glad to see him, and he me. We had developed a friendship over the years.

He took his work seriously, but he could not help but boast about his exploits—about how we almost caught him by accident the past year, etc, etc. We would laugh over all of that, he and I; and I would catalog the information behind the facade of smiles: the where, when and how. It was taking a long time, but he was giving away his method of operating. He took his work seriously, but so did I. Maybe he became at ease with me because he knew I was not smart enough to catch him. I did not need to be—he was smart enough for both of us.

Over time I learned that this guide was escaping our clutches because he was super cautious. Immediately prior to the season, he would carefully fly his favorite hunting areas on the Alaska Peninsula looking for signs of our stakeouts. He knew he might miss a camouflaged camp stuck back in the alders, but if he found fresh airplane tracks on a pumice patch, he simply would not hunt that area. And he avoided hunting near the beaches, knowing the tide would erase signs of one of our airplanes dropping off a stakeout placement. Besides, there were gaggles of airplanes along the beaches at any given moment during the hunting season.

In the watersheds he hunted, he built small cabins designated as his registered camps. He seldom placed anyone there to begin with and hunted directly out of the comforts of his lodge by airplane. His favorite method was to load up his Super Cub with a client and an assistant guide, fly the favored watersheds near where one of his cabins was located until he spotted a satisfactory bear, drop off his two passengers along with their gear, and then drive the bear to them with his Super Cub. After he was satisfied they had taken the bear, he would not land but would return to his lodge. The assistant guide would skin the bear, cover the carcass with grass and brush to discourage birds and wildlife troopers from spotting it, and he and the hunter would backpack, along with the hide, to the registered camp. There they would be picked up on the morrow by the guide. Although we suspicioned that he did this, he had never been caught nor ever been seen in the act by anyone who would be inclined to report him.

I decided to concentrate most of my available stakeouts on him one season. Knowing we would not be able to take them in by fixed-wing aircraft, leaving tracks for the guide to see, we would have to drop them off by helicopter; and the stakeouts would be there for the duration (up to three weeks possibly). We would need to pick them up by Super Cub when it was over. I couldn't tie up our Alaska State Trooper helicopter 500 miles from where it was needed most, around the busy crime area of Anchorage. The stakeouts would have to pack out to a place where we could land with an airplane.

I knew from visiting earlier with this guide when he would arrive in the hunting area that spring of 1980. He would be there three days before the season to open the lodge, prepare for the hunters, and scout the country for bear.

Five days before the fifteen-day season opened, we flew into our staging area south of the Meshik River. This was close enough to his hunting country to allow quick individual placement of six men with the fuel-gobbling helicopter. We flew into a large, remote pumice patch: six Super Cubs (each loaded with a stakeout and his three-week supply of gear and groceries), the helicopter, and our DeHavilland Beaver loaded with cases of fuel for the chopper. Eight pilots hustling to get the stakeouts placed one at a time into predetermined spots within the hunting areas of this bandit guide, all the time worrying about being seen by someone happening by and the word getting out. Fortunately, we were not seen and the placements went successfully.

Each of the stakeouts were provided with a single-sideband handy-talky which, when connected to an aircraft battery and strung-out antennae, could be used to talk to our main patrol camp at Pumice Creek, a distance of about eighty miles across the mountains. They would call in twice a day at predetermined times, careful to give names and locations by code only. The guide knew our frequencies and was one of the first to own a scanner.

⚬∾

Fifteen days go by after the stakeouts are put out. Nothing. The guide is seen in one or more of the areas each day, but there is no illegal activity. I begin to have doubts about the whole thing, and am apprehensive about the stakeouts' wellbeing as the weather has been tough: hundred-mile-an-hour winds on the Pacific side of the Alaska Peninsula where most of the stakeouts are located: rain, fog, and misery.

On the sixteenth day, Wildlife Trooper Dave Loring is blended into a high hillside overlooking the Ivan River valley when the guide flies low over him. Dave sees three people inside, and they seem to be looking right at him. He fears they have seen him, but they haven't. The plane flies low and slow, zigzagging its way up the valley and up around a mountain out of Dave's sight. Then it comes back down the valley and begins circling an area not too far from Dave's lookout. A bear has been spotted.

The plane lands on a gravel bar along the braided river and two people get out; then it takes off and circles high until the two on the ground get situated for a kill. Dave watches as the plane begins to swoop and dive, driving the bear to the hunters. He cannot see the bear in its final run, but he hears the reports of a rifle; and soon the plane leaves the area, heading back to the Bering Sea side of the mountains towards the lodge. Dave hikes down to the river and waits; he is between the hunters and the little registered camp they will use down the valley.

In a few hours, the assistant guide and the hunter stroll down the edge of the river packing a large brown bear hide and skull. They are shocked to run into Dave, who is dressed like a hunter, but immediately identifies himself.

As the three of them are talking, an airplane flies over. It is the guide, who quickly sees that there are now three people where he had left only two. He flies back to the lodge and immediately strips all the accessories off his plane: big tires, radios, navigational aids—preparing it for the seizure that he is smart enough to know is inevitable. He is smart enough to know that he has been caught; smart enough to know that he will not be picking up his hunter and assistant guide off the river, that he will be having his attorney bail them out of jail; and smart enough to know that when all of this is over, he will have to salvage what is left and maybe go into the fish guiding business where the stakes are not so high.

When we seized his Super Cub that day at his Wild Lake camp south of Port Heiden, he said, "I'd invite you in for coffee, but conversations have a way of ending up as court testimony, it seems." I agreed with him. Then he said, "You don't realize all the strain and stress there is in this business… you guys go home and sleep every night, while I stay awake most of the time worrying about if I'm going to get caught."

"Well," I said, "you might have tried hunting legally for a change, at least long enough to get some sleep."

PART FIVE: ENDINGS

"Knowledge comes but wisdom lingers."
— Alfred Lord Tennyson

CHAPTER TWENTY-SIX

The Broken Dragonfly

He dragged Wiltrout to the leeward side of the wreckage where they were out of the worst of the wind.

Wildlife Trooper Sergeant John Stimson has no idea his day off will be any different than the rest of them in the winter of 1982-83. He comes into the office, in the Prince William Sound town of Cordova, to finish some paperwork, but soon the phone rings and he's asked to help on a search for an overdue aircraft. A charter pilot flying alone from Cape Yakataga to Cordova in a single-engine Cessna 185 has radioed for help. She is low on fuel, the weather is blowing snow with poor visibility, and she's not sure of her exact position, only that she's somewhere on the Copper River Flats, twenty-five to thirty miles southeast of Cordova. The controller at the FAA Flight Service Station has been unable to re-contact her, and is certain she must now be down out there somewhere in the blizzard.

Stimson is the skipper of the "PV Enforcer," a sixty-five foot fisheries patrol vessel permanently stationed, along with its four-man crew, in Cordova. In John's career with the Marine Section of the Fish and Wildlife Protection Division, he has been on a lot of saltwater search and rescue operations in some of Alaska's most treacherous waters, including the Bering Sea. But those were fishing boats in distress, and this is a Prince William Sound land search. For John, this air/ground search for an airplane will make him feel somewhat like a fish out of water. He is asked to be an observer on a chartered helicopter due to leave as soon as he can get out to the airport. He drops what he is doing and goes.

City Police Chief Bill Bagron, sitting in his office near the front door of the building, has been keeping track of the search situation even though it's out of his jurisdiction. "Where're you headed, John?" he asks Stimson as he walks by in the hallway.

"To see if we can't find that lost pilot," are John's words as he heads out the door.

Bagron said he notices John is wearing only his jeans, leather boots, and a lightweight army parka. "It's snowing and blowing pretty hard out there, John," he calls after him. But John doesn't answer, and is gone.

Bagron said he didn't want to interfere with John's plans, but he knows that it's an unusually heavy storm—his own attempts to drive a four-wheel-drive out the Copper River Road to help in the search have been stopped by zero visibility and heavy snow drifts—and he just wants to prevent any unnecessary flying if he can.

∽

At the airport John climbs into the waiting Bell 206 chopper. He hasn't taken any of the precious time to retrieve his cold weather gear, and wears only his parka. Otherwise he is dressed in the light clothes of an indoor day off. The civilian charter pilot, Gary Wiltrout—a pilot of considerable flying experience—is dressed similarly. It is January 13th in Alaska, the coldest time of the year.

The Copper River Delta is an immense area of barren, featureless, sand flats and tidal guts, and today the snow driven by winds of seventy to ninety mph has reduced the visibility of this horizonless country to zero within seventy-five feet of the ground. John and Wiltrout peer through the frosted windscreen of the helicopter, searching the drifting snow and frozen sand directly beneath them for the downed airplane. They know that the young woman might freeze to death if they can't find her before dark. No one else is out searching in this stuff. They fly back and forth, a few hundred feet off the ground in a meandering grid from the coast toward the mountains. Then on a long, slow turn, the engine falters and quits.

"Mayday, Mayday...engine failure!" Wiltrout shouts over the radio, as he begins an auto-rotation to soften his landing and before he loses total sight of the ground due to the blizzard. It is the last radio transmission the

FAA Station in Cordova will receive from the chopper. It's only an hour till dark.

A year or so before, I had returned to state service and been transferred to the Kenai Peninsula as detachment commander. John's patrol area of Prince William Sound was in my area of responsibility. I was notified at home in Soldotna the night his helicopter was overdue. It was hoped they'd made it safely to the ground, but the worst was feared as there hadn't been any contact with them since the engine failure. Our Department of Public Safety helicopter crew in Anchorage was alerted to be ready to fly at daybreak, and a State Trooper search team was readied for a flight into Cordova. A U.S. Coast Guard H-3 helicopter prepared to depart at first light for the area, and a U.S. Air Force C-130 Search and Rescue aircraft had already left Anchorage.

John and Wiltrout found themselves thrown clear of the helicopter, which lay like a broken dragonfly in the blowing snow. The chopper had impacted the ground in a left, nose down attitude and rolled over. Later deduction by a National Transportation Safety Board investigation faulted the pilot for inadequate pre-flight examination. No mechanical engine failure was found, but a coating of ice was discovered in the engine inlet.

Wiltrout had a broken back. John wasn't injured, and he dragged Wiltrout to the leeward side of the wreckage where they were out of the worst of the wind. He couldn't force a way into the baggage area due to the twisted fuselage, trying again and again until well after dark, sapping his energy, fighting against a seventy mph wind with higher gusts and a chill factor of fifty below zero and lower. There were four sleeping bags and seven days' worth of survival rations in the helicopter, but John couldn't reach any of it.

Meanwhile, the Air Force C-130 had arrived in the dark, high above the storm, and established radio contact with the missing charter pilot. She had wrecked her Cessna on a sand bar, tearing off the landing gear and bending the propeller, but was alright, she told them. She was inside the fuselage with her emergency gear and could wait. She would have to, it would be a while. Later, NTSB faulted her for using poor judgment by entering adverse weather after being warned of significantly bad conditions. A hard pill to swallow for a flight instructor with almost 10,000 hours of flying time under her belt.

∽

John and Wiltrout huddled in the snow against their broken helicopter. They talked to each other through the long hours. "Let's take the next ride to town, shall we? I don't like it out here," John joked with Wiltrout, trying to bolster the other man's spirits. The two had never met before that day.

The weather worsened the next day; the wind increased, and the snowfall intensified. Late in the morning, however, the search was resumed, although the weather only seemed better by using some stretch of the imagination.

Then, shortly before noon, the Coast Guard helicopter spotted the wreckage of the chopper through the snow squalls and swirling mass of the ground blizzard. But they couldn't land due to some sort of hydraulic problems. However, the news they relayed back was good—they said they saw two people waving at them from the ground. The search command base in Anchorage let me know right away, and I telephoned John's aging mother, who lived in a Kenai rest home, of the good news.

About the ordeal of the night before, Wiltrout later said, "We got to know each other real well. We talked about everything from God, to the crash, to our families, to the miserable weather. We figured if we could hold out until morning, they would probably get us. I know John was worried that I wasn't going to make it because of my back...but I think the pain in my back kept me alert."

The talk between the two that night became less and less frequent; a wall of drifting snow had built up between them. "We had to yell a little louder each time," Wiltrout said. "The last time I remember talking to John was about seven in the morning. I said, 'John are you ready for breakfast?' He didn't answer. I tried to get up, but the snowbank had built up around me, and with my back, it took me thirty minutes to dig out of the snow with my hands. Finally I got out and found John. He was still sitting there beside me, but he had passed away by then."

By daylight the pilot, in spite of his pain, was able to locate a crack in the fuselage. He fished out two sleeping bags. It would be a lonely and vacant day for Gary Wiltrout.

Just before dark, the State Trooper helicopter, piloted by Bob Larson, arrived in the area and found both Wiltrout and the pilot of the missing Cessna. The two downed aircraft were less than two miles apart.

I've thought about that turn of events plenty of times. It was more than a false hope when John was reported alive; it was a relief of the entire physical and psychological systems—a calming of the anxiety that can build up in a twenty-four hour period of time. As it appeared at first, the worst case scenario did not happen. So you think: *Now, let's see if they can get them out of there safely; then we'll see how much they've suffered and what it will take for full recovery of any physical or mental injuries. If they were waving, that's the best sign for right now—they've survived!*

So I suppose, in that situation, if you are John's family and friends and co-workers, you let down your guard; you no longer have to mentally prepare yourself for something that may well be tragic. And if you are John's wife or John's mother, you can release that fear from its tight grip on you—like waking up from a nightmare in a cold sweat and being thankful to your god, or whatever might be out there in the dark night of the bedroom, saying it's alright, you were just dreaming. And whether you are consciously recollecting it or not, it's something that is calming; and although the nightmare is still vivid and frightening, you are grateful for the reprieve and for the truth that there is some goodness, and that all the nightmares in the world aren't real, and all the bad dreams don't come true.

For John Stimson's mother, I can only attest that the nightmare and worry of the last twenty-some hours were gone from her eyes when I walked into her little apartment to see her that night. I am thankful she had some of her friends still surrounding her at the rest home there in Kenai—friends still re-living and rejoicing with her the passing of the recent nightmare, and that her son had been found alive. In that fleeting instant of time, which lingered before I had to tell her that I was in error— that her son *was* gone—I wished that somehow I could simply capture forever the moment of happiness that shone on her face.

CHAPTER TWENTY-SEVEN

Flying Bricks and Boiled Shirts

The challenge of finding a landing place would get me in more trouble than just looking for caribou.

The runway at Santa Fe, New Mexico, where I learned to fly, is close to 7,000 feet above sea level. I didn't know then what the true performance of an airplane could be in the fat air at ocean level, never having experienced it, so when I moved to Alaska and made my first takeoff at close to sea level, I nearly let the airplane get away from me, it was so responsive. I was in the air less than half the normal distance down the runway, it seemed, and I wasn't ready for the high performance level.

My training in New Mexico was in the classic, nose-geared Cessna 150, but in Alaska I would need to learn to fly the tail-draggers in my job as a wildlife officer. The first hundred or so hours in Alaska skies were while flying a Super Cub from the passenger's rear seat, where there was another set of rudder pedals and controls. You couldn't see out of the thing when it was on the ground, and it must have been scary watching me zigzag down the runway trying to master directional control from the back seat, like some kid trying to ride a tricycle sitting backwards on it. By the time I put in over a hundred hours from the back (and by the time my buddy Jack gathered up enough nerve to trade places with me), the front seat was like an entirely new airplane—I could see down the runway, I could take off without wandering all over the weed patch, and there were instruments to look at up there.

Some years later, when I was a check pilot for the Department of Public Safety, among other things, and had developed a certain smugness, I suppose, and thought there wasn't a tail-dragger I couldn't handle, Garland Dobson showed up at the door with a newly purchased Piper Pacer. It was a short-coupled, narrow-geared, mean little airplane, one with a wing span considerably less than that of a Super Cub. We called the Pacers and Tri-Pacers "flying bricks" due to their engine-out gliding incapabilities.

Garland said, "I just flew this thing up from the lower forty-eight, and I guess I just don't have the right touch...it's almost uncontrollable on the ground." That comment in itself should have raised a red flag for me; Garland was an accomplished pilot. But cockiness can be impishly disguised as mild ego in one's own mind.

I said, "Shoot, let's take a look at it."

We went over to Merrill Field, the runway in the middle of Anchorage, got in the bunched-up little brick, taxied out to the active runway, and I shoveled the coal to it. The little airplane came so close to getting away from me that I still hate to visualize it—so close that Garland shouted, "Enough, enough! I'll figure the damned thing out for myself!" as I aborted the takeoff.

"Wait a minute—wait a minute," I said, "I want another shot at it...I guess I just wasn't ready that time."

So, reluctantly (on his part), we taxi a circuit back around to the active runway—the man in the control tower has no doubt taken an interest in this contest by now—and I shove the power in again, only this time I'm on top of it...for about a hundred feet, maybe less. We're dancing all over the runway—I didn't do this badly when I was a new pilot in the back seat of a Cub—and I almost stack it up before I jump it into the air and catch the little crosswind straight on, just short of a major ground loop. Garland, in the right seat, has been trying to take it away from me, to salvage what he can, and I'm shouting at him to keep his hands to himself. He's pretty red-faced about it: not embarrassed—*mad*. But we're in the air, and I fly around the pattern and land. Some crow-hopping and jig-sawing, but not too bad, I think, compared to the takeoff.

By the time we get back to the tie-down, though, Garland is smiling, probably just feeling glad to still have an airplane, but I don't like the look of the smile and tell him so, "What are you grinning at?" His smile just gets bigger. I get in the car and drive off; he can tie his own dumb airplane down. I knew what he was thinking: He was thinking he wasn't so bad at handling the Pacer after all, and he was glad it wasn't just his ability that was lacking. Or maybe he was just happy to still be alive.

I had a little respect though, after that, when I saw some young student pilots learning to fly in one of those narrow-geared flying bricks. As for me, I wouldn't touch one again for any amount of money.

∞

I left state service at one point in my career and started a guiding business for sport fishermen and hunters. While trying to establish some clientele, I guided hunters and flew a couple of years for Stan Frost, a master guide and outfitter. His hunting area was along the western slope of the Alaska Range, the lodge and headquarters sitting at the east end of Farewell Lake, one of the larger bodies of water on that side of the mountains.

Frost bunked his guides in an old cabin that was part of the property there—Einer Carlson's old homestead place. An ancient, cabinet-style radio was there that would pick up stations from all over the northern hemisphere late at night, and there were some old diaries from back in the late twenties and early thirties, the words being those of Carlson while on his trapline each winter. They started out with no mention of airplanes. Some of the entries were short. "Boiled the shirt," he wrote on days when the weather was too bad to go out, or when he felt like staying in for whatever reason.

Then, in '31 or '32, I think it was, he saw his first airplane while he was mushing along the South Fork of the Kuskokwim River, up near Hell's Gate. He talked as though this airplane was an apparition, or even an aberration; some newfangled something or other, not destined to stick. But in a few years he was writing about seeing more and more airplanes, and finally, after a while, he was talking about being hauled out to his trapline by an airplane; then it was about expecting a planeload of this or that, and why the hell was so-and-so two days late with that load of supplies? "Boiled the shirt."

∞

Aside from guiding for Stan, I was doing some flying for him, taking hunters and assistant guides into some short strips with his Super Cub and picking up supplies and clients in Anchorage and hauling them out to the lodge with his Cessna 180, a responsive bird that purred and was light on its toes. Stan never let anyone else fly his planes. He had the greatest confidence in me.

I almost didn't live up to Stan's expectations though. Earlier in the season I ran a tent pole through the fabric of the right wing of the Cub, thinking I knew, like you would know the ends of your fingers, the exact position, within six inches, of the wing tips sticking out there seventeen feet or so.

Then after that, Stan suggested I take the Cessna 180 over around the Lyman Hills, the other side of Big River, to see if I could find some caribou in that country, maybe somewhere between the Cheeneetnuk and Gagaryah rivers. We were getting short of caribou on the South Fork of the Kuskokwim. If I could locate a decent herd, maybe we would move a camp in there and hunt some new country. Stan said as far as he knew there weren't any good places to land, but maybe I could snoop around and locate a good spot nobody else had found.

The challenge of finding a landing place would get me in more trouble than just looking for caribou.

I burned up quite a bit of fuel looking the country over, to no avail; but before heading back without anything to show for the trip, I spotted a little bunch of caribou on some bald hills along the headwaters of the Gagaryah. The size of the herd wouldn't justify moving a camp in there, but I figured where there's smoke, you know, there might later be fire. The truth is the caribou gave me a semi-valid reason to hunt up a landing spot, which I was itching to do.

Looking the area over carefully—I knew there had to be a place to land there somewhere—I found what I took to be the answer in a big swale. It was a little snaky and in some rolling heaves of tundra, but I figured it would suffice. First, though, I would drag the area low and slow and get as near to a ground view as I could.

It looked a little rough, but I plunked it in at the last moment, even though I hadn't planned it that way. It just felt right for a fleeting second. I don't know if you've ever done that, something almost instinctual, and later wondered how your instincts could let you down so badly (you have to blame stupidity on something). You're not supposed to fly that way—doing something on the spur of the moment without taking some time to think about it, if there are other alternatives, anyway.

The very moment I committed to the landing and felt the contours of those tremendous bulges in the ground, the way the landing gear sprung and flounced and rebounded to the undulating swale, I knew I shouldn't have done it. I was cussing myself before I shut down the engine, before I climbed out and took a look at the endless mounds of earth, and before I saw the land's equivalent of an ocean's rip tide—jumbled earth in every direction, no continuity to the way the waves rolled. I would be lucky to even taxi in this place. *How the hell had I kept from busting a landing gear?* It spoke well for the tough, springy Cessna gear legs. This was four-wheeler country without any four-wheelers.

I began talking to myself in solid words—words some folks would find insulting. After chewing myself out to the best of my ability, I started talking about what I was going to do now, discussing the thing like I was two or three people maybe, arguing and muttering all the way across this mangled-looking, bloated landing strip I had discovered in my wisdom. The truth was, I was afraid; but I didn't want to think about being afraid, so I stayed mad at myself to ease the pain; talked to myself and remonstrated myself like I was my old man (or how I remembered his sounding sometimes when he caught me being dumb).

There was a ridge that strung out toward the higher hills; I headed for it. At least I could look at the lay of the land from up there.

After climbing up the hill, it seemed that the only half-way smooth terrain around was on this ledge. Only it was stair-stepped, a few hundred feet or so of flat area, then a drop off—a steeper grade, anyway—down to another flat spot. I eyeballed the country around. There was nothing else. I figured if I took it easy, I could taxi the plane—three-wheel it out across the rolling heaves and up the ridge. Maybe I was dreaming, I thought. Maybe I was hoping for something that wasn't possible, and maybe this would have been a better day to have stayed in camp and boiled the shirt.

I trotted back to the plane, taking notice of how it sat there looking uncomfortable tipped to one side, imagining that it seemed to have an expectant look, like it was wondering if I had found a good place, and, like a child, totally trusting my judgment.

I carefully drove it over the hummocks and up the ridge, getting a run on the flat spots so I wouldn't have to power it so hard up the steps. Then when I reached the longest flat, I swung it around at the far end and shut it down. I wanted to size everything up again with the presence of the airplane in the picture, maybe hoping that the airplane could take a look at it, and give me an idea if it could be done. I talked to the plane and to myself some more, as though to give us both confidence.

Poor Stan.

Checking the elevation, I considered the temperature for density altitude, the amount of fuel used up, and tested the wind, which was as calm as a south sea island. I prayed for a little breeze up the slope. I stepped off the length of the flat, and looked down to the next bench; it was quite a bit shorter.

To make this thing work—this takeoff—I would need to have enough flying speed to give the plane some buoyancy at the edge. I knew there wouldn't be enough speed gathered in the short distance I had to keep the airplane in the air after I got off the ground. But if there was adequate lift generated by the time I reached that first edge, I could sort of float down to the next bench, which should increase my speed a little, and bounce it off, ricochet it, gather a handful of flaps, and hope to stay in the air because the next bounce wouldn't be a bounce.

The whole idea stunk. It stunk because there were too many variables, none of which I knew for certain would work. It wasn't as if I could abort the takeoff at a go or no-go place along the path. If there was not enough speed at the end of the flat, then the plane would drop off and crunch into the ground nose first, down on the next bench. Or even if it lacked a little bit of enough speed and just sank on me, I would hit the lower bench too hard and bust the gear. All these things were racing through my mind, and there was that cottony texture in my mouth, and the taste of metal on my tongue, a taste I've had only a few times in my life. It's the taste of business-like fear.

I waited patiently for sometime, savoring the living moments, smoking what might be my last cigarette (like a blindfolded prisoner about to hear the final orders to the firing squad), but all the while dreading the thing I was about to do. I wanted the wind to pick up, any breeze at all from the right direction. Soon I imagined a breeze, and jumped in the plane and cranked it up, then re-thought my nerve, shut it down again, got out and waited some more. I soon felt another whiff of air from down the slope, hopped in, cranked it up, pulled a notch of flaps, firewalled it with brakes on tight, then released them and let 'er go.

She felt light by the time I reached the edge of the step. I didn't try to lift it off, just flew it out and down to the next bench, where I bounced it off lightly, the spring-gear twanging in reverberation, and grabbed another notch of flaps to gain some more lift, like holding the plane in the air by sheer muscle, working the flaps for a feel of buoyancy, bleeding them off as we gained speed, the engine and prop at full air-sucking power. We were flying, by God!

CHAPTER TWENTY-EIGHT

A Family Outing

You like to think that you are a safe pilot. So when you commit some act that is abhorrent to what you expect of yourself, it's like being struck by a mallet with stupidity written all over it.

The first car I ever drove solo, I kept looking around inside just for the reassurance I was truly alone and herding the thing down the road by myself. I could run off the road if I wanted—nobody would yell at me or say anything, at least not at that moment, anyway. It was a wonderful feeling to know I had control of a big piece of machinery.

The first time I soloed an airplane I was too busy to enjoy the luxury of gloating. That came later, on my first cross-country flight, when there was more time to think about being up in the sky in a piece of metal without a parachute and no one to boss you around. Then it wasn't thinking about how I had the option to crash if I wanted; the thoughts were more prideful, knowing I knew how to get out of this predicament without help from an instructor (the predicament being the act of flying). I suppose anything you learn to do that is out of character has similar feelings of how incredible it is. Then as you become accustomed to what you've learned, you become somewhat complacent about it—like old hat. That's where the danger lies in flying. Or even driving a car, for that matter.

That first year driving a car, I had three wrecks. Wrecks, not just fender-benders. It was different later with flying. Maybe the difference was the attitude that develops between fifteen years old and thirty years old.

Learning the importance of self-preservation was part of it, maybe—recognizing the possibility of dying. But I also had a pride in not wanting to tear up an airplane entrusted to me. When I finally did demolish an airplane, it was my own. Busting up your own airplane has a way of getting your attention.

There's a pride all pilots have which I will admit to. We like to believe we're good at what we do. It's not that each pilot thinks he's better than the rest, that's not what I mean; it's a pride in reaching a certain individual plateau, and if you are comfortable with that point of progress, you become defensive of it. You like to think that you are a safe pilot too—that goes with it. So when you commit some act that is abhorrent to what you expect of yourself, it's like being struck by a mallet with "stupid" written all over it.

The subject is not something new, but it's a thing I need to talk about here, for myself, if nobody else. It's a way of saying you can't afford to make dumb mistakes when flying; most important when you have passengers, and more important still, when the passengers are your family. The pride says we never make mistakes—they are not allowed—and if we use bad judgment with someone on board we especially care about, it's unforgivable. The protective side of us establishes that it's not acceptable.

∽

I bought a 1947 Stinson 108-3 in 1974. It was truly a beautiful airplane. Totally rebuilt inside and out, it was striking in its cream and chocolate color scheme, its elegant polished mahogany and pleated leather interior, its sweeping droop-tipped wings, its skirted gear and tight, drumming fabric. It sat low to the sod in a sort of comfortable demure like an old refurbished, burnished Cadillac.

I thought of myself then as an accomplished Cessna 180 pilot. I suppose I could look up the number of hours I had logged by that stage of my progress, but it wouldn't make the point any clearer. I thought of myself in that way, and it might be true. I would have preferred a one-eighty rather than the Stinson, but I couldn't afford one. The Stinson is what we pilots called a poor-man's one-eighty, the only similarity being it is a high wing, single-engine, four-place airplane with adequate baggage space. This Stinson's 190 h.p. Franklin engine and airframe design would never compare in performance to the more recently designed 180 Cessna with its 230 h.p. Continental engine, though I suppose the Stinson Station Wagon, as the company called it, was the ultimate answer to a family airplane just after the second big war. But it was never the bush airplane that the name Stinson evokes—the name signifying images of the old bush freight hauler, the famous radial-engined Gull Wing Stinson of significantly more horses.

I flew the Stinson Station Wagon up to Alaska from Shreveport, Louisiana, where I bought it, and must have had about sixty hours in it by the time I hopped the family out to a little makeshift camp we set up on Lake Creek, a wilderness trout stream a hundred miles west of Anchorage. The gravel bar was plenty long enough, and was the only good place to land on wheels throughout the entire middle length of Lake Creek. A perfect spot, I figured. It was golden-leaf fall and the bugs had been knocked down by early frosts. The water of this large creek was a bright clear that time of year. The older kids could walk a little way down to the point and catch and release rainbows and Dolly Varden, or bring a mess back for breakfast, lunch, or supper—we couldn't get our fill of fried fish.

The second day out turned off rainy, but it didn't bother us. We fished, hiked the wet woods and hills with rubber boots and slickers on (the Alaskan way of summer day-hiking), picked blueberries, hunted up wood, and kept a multi-log fire blazing out front of the big lean-to, keeping wet clothes smoky dry.

The creek began to rise.

This gravel bar we were camped on—we were nestled into the willows along its highest level—this bar was actually a dry gravel fork of the creek, or at least a large part of the landing area was. So when creek water began to show in the low spots, I gave it some thoughtful notice throughout the day, but soon could see that the level remained constant over a period of eighteen hours or so. I was comfortable with that, but in the late hours of the following evening, I could see the stream had taken a change, and was now beginning to run in several new places and show a certain murkiness, the worst place being a relatively low spot about halfway down the only takeoff area I had. I experienced a twinge of thinking that I might have been foolish not to leave earlier in the day, but now it was almost dark, so I could do nothing but wait for morning.

By morning the trickle was close to a foot deep where it crossed the gravel wash, and a significant distance across. It left me only a marginal length of the upper end for takeoff, enough for a Cessna 180 with half tanks of fuel and a medium load; but the Stinson? I didn't know for sure. I'd crank it up and take a feel of it by myself first.

It felt good, and I took off, flew around the patch and landed. Not bad. It gave me confidence. I would take my wife and baby and the two younger kids, a little emergency gear, and leave the older boys and the camp for later—they were teenagers and woods savvy.

A Cessna 180 has four notches of flaps. The first two are best for takeoff (the lower flap configurations of three and four notches are normally used only for short, slow landings). You can manually give yourself a little lift on a short takeoff in the two-notch (half-flaps) position, adding a bit more flap by hoisting the handle a skosh, sort of like lifting yourself up by the bootstraps for that added flotation needed, then bleeding it off after the obstacles are cleared, allowing the airplane to build speed. The Stinson, on the other hand, has only two notches of flaps (the flaps are much smaller), the first notch (half-flaps) for takeoff, the second (full flaps) position for landing short. The truth is, the second notch serves as more of a spoiler; in other words, its ability to add lift on takeoff is doubtful, if not detrimental, as it turns out.

I had confidence, after my solo run, and felt some sort of infallibility in the decision to go with that particular load. I must have, although in hindsight it's much easier to just say I was stupid. Maybe that's the way you die sometimes—stupid, and with no opportunity for hindsight. Or maybe you don't die, but someone else does—someone who trusts your decisions; and if that's the case, then you are still stupid, but you have to live the rest of your life with the agony of that particularly bad decision.

In this case, nobody died, but I know they could have, except for luck or something of higher understanding and forgiveness. To this day, no one in my large family has ever mentioned the incident. Maybe that is a denial that it ever happened. Or maybe a respect for my own silence on the matter—just let me live with it or talk about it or deny that it took place or that I could make such a dumb move. They could all out-wait me on it. There's no reason to have to fly "on a wing and a prayer" as they say—that was during the war, for those souls who had no choice. Here, it's from a bush wing: You make good choices if you are to be a lasting bush flyer; and while it is in the raw bush where ideas might plead innovation, you take the time to make good decisions. You must always be sure of the outcome.

༄

The run-up was a repeat of before—no reason to feel differently about this takeoff—everything looked good. There was something else though: The two older boys watching from the side of the runway were apprehensive for some reason. They had witnessed my earlier takeoff—a simple, correct maneuver. So, why now the apprehension? Could they detect a doubt in me, one that I couldn't admit to myself? I've gone over and over that decision, all the pre-flight, all the thoughts leading up to the attempt. They trusted my decision and my abilities. I trusted, too.

The Stinson never gained the speed I needed. It was one of those takeoffs where it's full-speed ahead. No halfway point where you decide to abort, where an abort means winding up in the water off the little bank of the gut that had cut its way across the runway. It was a full-throttled go-for-it. When I reached the crossing, I naturally grabbed for the flap handle to give it that added boost—pop it into the air, this poor-man's 180. But there was no help from this boost of flaps. I remember the plane just running off into the creek, the creek grabbing the tires like a thick layer of glue spread across in front a foot deep, the water blowing up into the sky outside, and the world turning over inside—a slow motion of hang time while we turned a somersault over onto our backs. It wasn't at all like Little Underhill Creek, where God just lifted the plane back into the air; this time it was going over, and there wasn't a sound made by the children, Cindy and Charlie, wide eyed in the back seat, only some quiet cry of disbelief from my wife, who had the baby in her arms.

There wasn't any turmoil of screaming kids or crying baby. There was just silence and hot-engine-in-water sounds. No noisy 190 horsepower Franklin engine—it was dead. My first thought was to get everyone out of there, but I couldn't move: the trim crank handle attached to the ceiling, now part of the bottom of the creek, was hung up inside the back of my shirt collar. I expected fire, and felt a helpless panic. I knew more than anyone we needed to get out of there ("Get out! Get out!" I shouted), yet I couldn't move myself, like in a bad dream when you are trying to run, but your legs won't work. I called for Charlie, my twelve-year-old in the back seat, to help break me loose. He carefully untangled my collar. I think now that any ordinary person, especially a child, would be clambering to get out of that place—an upside down world with creek water running through the roof of the cockpit, and steam boiling out of the hot engine, and your father shouting for everyone to get out. Not Charlie. Whether he feared my wrath for failing to respond, or possessed a special presence of mind in a crisis, I don't know; possibly both. Regardless, with a cool determination he stayed and worked my collar loose. Then we were all out. There were no physical injuries, only damage to my pride and confidence.

We would go out again, all of us, within a year's time, on to another gravel bar, this time on the upper Talkeetna River for a week, and with a different airplane. It had to be. The fear needed to be faced and overcome, with some wisdom added.

CHAPTER TWENTY-NINE

Attitudes

If I were to pin good and bad flying down to one word, I think attitude would cover it (the configuration of the airplane in the air is not what I mean here).

Rain mixed with snow has reduced the visibility. I think about the old Cessna 195's with their narrow slits for a windscreen up front, and then I think about the Ryan that Lindbergh flew across the Atlantic in 1927, no windscreen at all, like a bullet with a little porthole along the side from which to see the world, and a periscope to see forward. The Cessna 180 I'm flying doesn't seem so bad after all, but the panel is up so high you would think all the manufacturer cares about is what you can see inside, not what's outside. I guess the grand view from a Piper Super Cub has spoiled me. Throw a little rain on the plexiglass, and some gray clouds, scud, and soup around you, and you really don't have good visibility out the front of a Cessna 180. But, like pilots of old, you learn to look at the important things, like the scenery, out the sides, and bore on through at 130 miles an hour in a semi-casual manner.

I became a lousy automobile driver after several years of flying the bush. I would catch myself driving along, herding the car down the road, and spending most of my time looking out the side window at the scenery.

Here in the Cessna 180, the visibility is strained, the rain mixed with snow, and mountains around shrouded in the silk of clouds. The beauty of the out-of-focus greens and yellows of fall stare out from the gray in between the scudded atmosphere, and though you concern yourself with what's up ahead, you can't help but notice the loveliness out the side as you pass a waterfall off to the left or a hanging blue-fissured glacier on the right while coming through Lake Clark Pass. As the forward visibility deteriorates through the canyon, you begin to check out the landing possibilities along the braided river below. Not that you're planning to land at that moment, it's for coming back to. A good habit.

As you move ahead, you pick out another good gravel bar—there's one I can come back to—knowing that the farther you proceed, and the worse the weather gets, there's a distinct possibility that it will close in behind you. So you work your way through in that manner, one good landing spot at a time, and if you're careful, you memorize the reciprocal of the heading you're on. If you find yourself suddenly in the soup, you don't want to waste time figuring it out: East and south (meaning 001 degree to 180 degrees on the compass): add 200 and subtract 20 from your present heading. West and north (meaning 181 degrees to 360 degrees on the compass): add 20 and subtract 200. You get used to working practicals in your head while you're flying along on good days; then on bad-weather days, you know how it works without thinking about it so much: Heading = 220, what's the reciprocal? Add 20, equals 240, take away 200, leaves 40. Reciprocal is zero-four-zero. Heading = 065, what's the reciprocal? Add 200, equals 265, take away 20, makes it 245. Reciprocal is two-four-five degrees.

&

In pilot's lingo in Alaska, there is what we call the "moose stall." It's a common phenomenon in the fall of the year. It can happen to either old cautious, or young bold pilots. It's when you get caught up in looking at a moose on the ground—or any other object for that matter—while in low, slow, tight, steep-banked, circling turns. You can forget all you ever learned about aerodynamics momentarily, and momentarily forgetting can kill you. You run out of airspeed, altitude, and ideas all at the same time, as they say, while the plane breaks into a sharp, wingover stall and spins nose down into the hard, unforgiving earth.

The FAA is always looking for new, innovative ways to curb the accident ratios. Unfortunately, it's usually with more laws, more regs, and more restrictions. Yet, it may be more unfortunate that the pilot's medical certificate doesn't require a psychological evaluation. The errors in just about all general aviation and air taxi accidents lay with the pilot. Of course, we pilots don't like to admit it ourselves, and we get tired of hearing other folks say it—aircraft mechanics, insurance adjusters, plane builders, the FAA, the media. But it's true, we're the ones.

If I were to pin good and bad flying down to one word, I think attitude would cover it (the configuration of the airplane in the air is not what I mean here). If you don't have a certain psychological disposition toward your flying abilities or inabilities, if there isn't a certain maturity there, you may be in for some miseries—you and any innocent passengers along. A non-pilot can relate to this; there's no great mystery to flying. Flying is a learned skill, like running a lawnmower in a responsible manner or driving a car safely. There's more studying, but you don't need to qualify as an astronaut to fly.

Many of us start driving a car as teenagers with a know-it-all, daredevil attitude. Mechanical and reflex ability we have, correct attitude we don't. You can't do that with an airplane. An airplane is not as forgiving as a car or a lawnmower. Some of the best pilots in Alaska are those raised in the bush; also some of the deadest—teenagers who started out in airplanes instead of cars, but nevertheless with a cocky attitude. Even though it's a demeanor more common to youth, there are some forty-year-olds out there flying right now with that attitude.

The most outstanding pilots I've known were ones who didn't feel they had something to prove, stuck to the safe side of what they knew their limitations were, didn't push the weather without knowing they had a safe way out, and took pride in their safety record, yet didn't brag about their prowess with an airplane.

Unfortunately, some of the celebrity pilots in Alaska were some of the worst. They were lucky if they survived. Bragging about the number of wrecks you walk away from doesn't improve your reputation. The listeners may nod and smile and stand in awe, while in the meantime they have decided they don't ever want to fly with you. George Custer had a lot of horses shot out from under him over the years in his wild and daring charges. (How do you feel about that now, George?...George?)

We pilots are often accused of being prima donnas. I've thought about that at length and decided the title was well-deservedly placed on flyers during World War One. In that war—the first where aircraft were used (not counting the six airplanes used against Pancho Villa by Blackjack Pershing's troops prior to that; they didn't come back out of Mexico)—the pilots flew out and engaged the enemy, then flew back (if lucky enough to fly back) to their home aerodrome where they allegedly drank champagne and chewed on caviar to celebrate their victories. Meanwhile, the ground troops were holed up in their foxholes contracting trench mouth, trench foot, or being gassed. Thus, they had some well-chosen names for the flyers, the least of which was "prima donna," no doubt.

Before that, there was the cavalry. The foot soldiers resented the cavalry for the same reason during the Civil War and the Indian Wars—fast, more comfortable travel, with the ability to return to a convenient camp at the end of a foray. Flamboyancy didn't help the image either: feather in the hat, high-topped boots, capes billowing in the wind. For the early pilots, it was the silk scarf trailing, then it was the leather jacket. Now, it's the big wristwatch with all the dials and the correct sunglasses.

The same thing could be said of World War II as the other wars, I suppose, and thus of any other profession wherein aircraft came into use, replacing horses, while there were unfortunates left behind on the ground.

I've known the feeling while guiding hunters: the registered guide dropping in for a few moments to check on the progress of the hunt while the assistant guide (me) does the ground work—the guiding of the client on his hunts; the skinning, fleshing, and the packing; the cooking, dishwashing, and babysitting associated with such a project (if you've been there, you know what I mean). You come away with a sour taste in your mouth for the guide/pilot, who within a few enjoyable airborne moments is back at the base camp or lodge where the cook is preparing the evening's gourmet fare, and it's time for the afternoon sip of Jose Cuervo. Prima donna.

In game warden work, it's the pilot/trooper versus the stakeout left out in the woods with the bears and the elements. Same thing.

Once you've experienced flight in lieu of shank's mare, you don't want to go back to foot or horse, or even car travel. I was already a pilot when I moved to Alaska in 1969. Before I was graduated to flight status with the Fish and Game Department, I was stuck with a Ford station wagon, a snowmachine, a borrowed riverboat, rented horses, and occasionally my own two feet—good accommodations compared to my great-grandfather's walking shoes and bare feet while tromping up and down the Shenandoah Valley with Stonewall Jackson's army.

But, none of these other means of travel was satisfactory. I was spoiled. When I rented three horses—two to pack, and one to ride—for a two-week patrol of the sheep season in the Alaska Range east of Mount McKinley National Park, I was at home, so to speak, traveling in the manner I was accustomed to on my better days in New Mexico. But I knew that if I had a Department airplane, I could check all the country in one day that it took me a week to ride through on horseback, including stopping in at the camps. I wasn't happy without an airplane, yet I was doing what I had treasured the most for many years: horse patrol. Once I traded the saddle for a Super Cub, there was no going back: cavalry straight to the Air Force.

༄

In flying, you must always leave a way out. That's what I tell anyone who will listen. Admittedly, I've been in bad situations where I thought I was doing that, but it didn't turn out the way I planned. But leaving a way out is a good policy. That's because you care about yourself, and those with you. I figure flying into a questionable weather situation, not knowing for sure if you can get out, is like Russian roulette—counting on an empty chamber to be there. It's one of the surest ways of dying. I'm too chicken to do that.

A hole up there in the overcast, with blue sky as a backdrop, is a sucker hole (So, you get up there—now what?). A hole down there where you can see the tempting earth, is another sucker hole if you're above the clouds looking to get down (maybe the hole does just that, goes all the way to the ground). Not knowing what you're getting into is akin to a trial attorney's asking a question he doesn't know the answer to. But the attorney only has his client's case to lose.

I knew a state trooper who would punch a hole up through the clouds when the weather got a little nasty down underneath—would punch up and go on instruments, often while flying a single-engine aircraft. He felt comfortable in that mode; something of a daredevil, he was. I worried about the people who rode with him; he seldom went anywhere alone. He's dead now, rolled himself up in a metal coffin on a hillside. He was close to a nice retirement and left a wife wondering what the hell it all meant; took another trooper out with him. His passengers trusted him, depended on his caring about their lives.

I think we squeak by sometimes, and the next thing, we know it all. We're secure in our knowledge about a given weather condition—*Oh, yeah, I've seen this before*—and we let our guard down. We're scared as hell when we start flying if we have any sense. We're cautious by the book. Then, as it is with human nature, we push our limits, like the little kid who keeps edging farther away from the house, and we feel a security in our own experiences. Maturity of attitude is something beyond that.

༄

There is no "last of the bush pilots." As long as there are airplanes and people to fly them, there will be bush pilots. The young men and women we see nowadays are no different than the ones before; it's like suggesting there are no more cowboys—some of the paraphernalia is different, but the heart, the need, and the desire are still alive. And the dangers are still there.

In fact, the risks may be higher now. In the air taxi business, for example, the client expects to get there right now; people are used to schedules and accustomed to the timeliness of those schedules. There's pressure on the pilot to produce for the company, and for the company to meet the same deadlines as the competition. It was somewhat that way in the beginning, I'm sure; however, there were no standards already established, much less expected.

I flew for a sport fishing lodge one summer when I was guiding for a living—a large state-of-the-art lodge in the Wood River-Tikchik Lakes area north of Dillingham. I leased my own airplane, a Cessna 206 on floats, which matched the two planes that Bob Curtis had (another 206 and a De-Havilland Beaver).

The country was new to me. Bob was fair, and said, "If you don't feel comfortable with the weather on any given day, don't fly...I'm not going to pressure you." That's what any good air taxi owner or guide should say to his pilots. But there's an unwritten or unsaid part of it too. What does a pilot do when his competitors or his compatriots fly, but he doesn't think the weather's good enough? At Tikchik Lodge, Bob and the other pilot loaded up their share of the clients and left on those days that looked pretty snotty to me. Do you think I was going to sit out the weather with my four or five fishermen, who were usually part of the same group, while these four or five knew their buddies were dragging in trophy rainbows over on the Togiak or Agulukpak rivers? I went, and usually went soon enough to keep the tail strobe on Bob Curtis' Beaver in sight up ahead in the scud. So, it's like a disclaimer—Don't fly when it's against your better judgment. (But the unsaid part is: If you don't fly, I may have to find another pilot.) In my case, there were other options—use the boat, or the motorized raft, or let them fish from the bank right at the lodge. Nothing would have been said, I'm sure. But in a lot of cases, especially in air taxi work, the customer goes next door.

Now, I say to you, let them go.

EPILOGUE

The eagle then made another pass, coming in with the sun behind him to blind his approach, like a fighter pilot diving to the kill.

Common loons build their nest each year in a cove along the shoreline at our cabin near Talkeetna, Alaska. Floating islands are there, perfect for the occasion, small vegetative masses which spring from the lake bottom, the floor of a tundra bog not too many years ago. None of the islands is over four feet across, and unattached to the shoreline of the lake, they are natural nesting sites for loons. These small lakes won't accommodate more than one pair of loons, or should I say, the loons won't allow it. Territorial. Each year they raise one or two chicks successfully, an accomplishment topped off in the fall by an airborne display of family unity—circling the perimeter of the lake, engrossed in some great preparation for winging south.

༄

    A pilot can't help but be fond of these other things that fly: birds and butterflies—you feel a kinship with them. You attach an airplane around yourself and you suppose you're one of them. The airplane becomes a part of you, as though you've opened up from an egg or a metamorphosed caterpillar maybe. You're in the air, and you've become something you've always wanted to be. The bounds and boundaries are lifted, and you feel a connection with those other winged creatures, and now assume something exists between you. It's a dimension that you can't experience anywhere else. The nearest to it may be the sensation of swimming under water with fish and porpoises; there's that other axis of movement that a pair of legs on the ground cannot produce. Multi-dimensional, fluid suspension: moving up, back, down, sideways—remaining stationary while floating in space. If you're a diver, you and the helicopter have something in common with the trout and the hummingbird.

This fondness for certain flying acquaintances may not be one-sided. Birds want to congregate near airplanes, like owls and sparrows and swallows nesting in old hangars, ducks and geese nesting along the shoreline on busy float plane marinas, gulls resting on seaplane tail feathers. Can they identify with something there? The other side of it, of course, is that we've roosted our airplanes in bird habitats, the nooks and crannies of waterways, or created nesting structures which meet with their approval. A hundred foot hangar is a swallow's house to a barn owl, I suppose.

I doubt though that owls and geese and gulls feel a kinship to these mechanical monstrosities once they roar to life with noise, turbulence, and belching fumes.

There's a particular eagle I remember who carried no fondness for metal birds. I was flying a Super Cub on floats along the upper Kuskokwim River, a few miles below the abandoned village of Vinasale downriver from McGrath. The river flows slow and easy through that part of the country. It was a sunny day, and I caught a flicker of shadowed movement off the left side of the airplane, a bald eagle's shadow against the opaqueness of the river. I saw him just as he struck the water, apparently after a fish, which is not unusual. This eagle, however, didn't hit the water and fly on with a fish in its talons. He stayed in the water, wings outstretched, floating with the current. I thought he must be a goner, but he slowly began to breaststroke with his wings toward the shore some twenty yards away. The drawback an eagle has when catching fish is that the talons lock onto the prey, but can't be released until the eagle settles his weight onto a solid surface. I circled and watched, looking, I suppose, like some vulture hoping for leftovers.

The eagle eventually reached the shore and hopped up on the land with a fish in his clutches. It was about a five pound fish, by the looks of it, but I couldn't tell what kind it was; too small to be a salmon, I figured. I circled back, dropped down, landed on the water, and taxied toward where the eagle was perched. Startled, he released the fish, which then proceeded to flop toward the water and struggled on into the river before I could get there to see what it was.

The eagle by then had flown atop a nearby white spruce. I took off and flew back by at about eye level with him as he sat there glaring back at me in disgust. Disgust best describes both his and my sentiments under the circumstances. I chastised myself for my greedy curiosity. It's tough enough for a sky bird like the eagle to have to swim for his lunch, without having a bigger bird—one with a thirty-five-foot wing span—come by and cheat him out of it.

If a bird, I'd be a loon,
Sleek, with ribboned checks of white,
Diving to depths in shades of
green, and winging across the
summer moon....

Eagles and loons. I spent the entire summer and fall once at our Talkeetna cabin and learned a little of the language of loons there. It wasn't that I intentionally did so, I just became used to hearing them in the background and grew accustomed to their calls of calm and sounds of alarm. So, I knew something was up when I heard the loons squawking in alarm one afternoon.

From the porch I could see they were swimming in tight circles and raising a ruckus. I grabbed my binoculars and eased down to the shore. The two adults were looking to the sky and were protesting loudly. About then a bald eagle flew low over them, making a single pass. I wondered about their two chicks, but couldn't see where they had gone. I knew they were never left alone anywhere. At that tiny fluff-ball size of only a few weeks old, they were always with one or both of the adults; but now it appeared they were gone. They were too young to dive.

It was the first year for the common loons to nest on the lake. The Arctic (now called Pacific) loons who were there previously had no luck raising their young over several seasons, and I always suspicioned eagles of snatching them up, so naturally, I imagined these little commons had met the same fate.

Then I saw them both. They were next to the adults—the adults still attentive to the sky. I was certain I hadn't missed them before. The eagle then made another pass, coming in with the sun behind him to blind his approach, like a fighter pilot diving to the kill. I noticed once again that the chicks were nowhere in sight. They were hiding underneath the adults' feathers where they were safe.

∽

Later, in the fall, I watched one of the loons teaching a fledgling to fly. She taxied downwind on the lake, giving herself a lot of room, the young one alongside. She turned into the wind and ran up the lake a ways flapping her wings...*pit, pit, pitting* along on her feet for a distance, then splashing to a stop and waiting. The young one flapped his wings and ran a few steps clumsily. She came coasting back, and did it again. He tried again. Several times they did this, until he got tired or bored or aggravated and started diving for stickleback minnows, which was more promising.

But in a week or so, she had him flying. The smaller fledgling was left alone each day for a time while the two adults and the other youngster flew around the perimeter of the lake, up high and moving fast and talking all the time. The smaller chick would yowl and carry on, and then after a bit, flap her wings and run into the wind to no avail. But a day or so later she had joined them, and they were all flying around the lake boundary, high and noiseless except for the whistling of their wings.

Flight.

Made in the USA
Charleston, SC
29 July 2012